Found...
Wor...

GCSE
Geography
for WJEC B

Andy Owen and Angela Calvert

DYNAMIC LEARNING

HODDER
EDUCATION
AN HACHETTE UK COMPANY

The Publishers would like to thank the following for permission to reproduce copyright material:

Photo credits

p.14, p.47, p.49, p.59 *all* © Andy Owen; **p. 40** © blickwinkel/Alamy.

Every effort has been made to trace all copyright holders, but if any have been inadvertently overlooked the Publishers will be pleased to make the necessary arrangements at the first opportunity.

Although every effort has been made to ensure that website addresses are correct at time of going to press, Hodder Education cannot be held responsible for the content of any website mentioned in this book. It is sometimes possible to find a relocated web page by typing in the address of the home page for a website in the URL window of your browser.

Hachette UK's policy is to use papers that are natural, renewable and recyclable products and made from wood grown in sustainable forests. The logging and manufacturing processes are expected to conform to the environmental regulations of the country of origin.

Orders: please contact Bookpoint Ltd, 130 Milton Park, Abingdon, Oxon OX14 4SB. Telephone: (44) 01235 827720. Fax: (44) 01235 400454. Lines are open 9.00–5.00, Monday to Saturday, with a 24-hour message answering service. Visit our website at www.hoddereducation.co.uk

© Andy Owen and Angela Calvert 2013
First published in 2013 by
Hodder Education,
An Hachette UK company
338 Euston Road
London NW1 3BH

Impression number   5 4 3 2 1

Year   2017 2016 2015 2014 2013

Cover photo © Mira/Alamy

Illustrations by Integra Software Services Pvt. Ltd

Typeset in 12 on 14pt ITC Stone Sans Medium by Integra Software Services Pvt. Ltd., Pondicherry, India

Printed by Hobbs the Printers, Totton, Hants

A catalogue record for this title is available from the British Library

ISBN: 978 14441 80 527

Contents

How to use this book

Welcome to this Geography workbook! It has been designed to be used alongside the *GCSE Geography for WJEC B Student's Book*. You will need a copy of the Student's Book open in front of you every time you use it. The Student's Book is full of maps, graphs, photographs and diagrams. This workbook bases its activities around these images.

The workbook is arranged in double pages. Each double page aims to tackle one or two geographical ideas, concepts or case studies. Sometimes the aim is to improve a geographical skill, such as using a map to describe a location. These aims are given as bullet points at the top of the left hand page in each spread.

There is another important piece of information that you will need before you can start any activity in this workbook. You will need to study the pages in the Student's Book. These page numbers are given in the top right of each left-hand page of the workbook.

You can write your answer to a lot of the activities in this workbook on the pages themselves. There are also some spaces to record other kinds of answers such as labelling sketches or drawing graphs. In this way you will gradually build up a set of notes and drawings that cover a large part of your GCSE Geography course. However, there isn't space in this book for all of your notes! You will need to keep a notebook too. This will be useful for your own notes. You will certainly need to use your own notebook for longer pieces of writing. The activities where you need to record an answer in your own notebook are signposted with a symbol of a pencil ✎.

It's good to keep lists and to tick off targets as you achieve them. We have, therefore, included a learning review at the end of each double page. These boxes quite often include simple steps but do tick them off. Add them altogether and you will see how much progress you can make over the two years you study GCSE Geography.

I hope you will find the workbook a useful way to organise your notes and test your understanding as you work your way through this GCSE Geography course.

Challenges of Living in a Built Environment

What different types of housing tenure are there?

See Student's Book pages 2–3

In these activities you will:

■ investigate the advantages of different types of housing tenure.

1 Complete Figure A. Use information from the boxes below.

How it works

A You sign a contract with a landlord who owns the property. You make regular payments for an agreed length of time (often six months). You pay a deposit to make sure you look after the property.

B You own a property or are in the process of buying one. Most people borrow the money from a mortgage lender, for example a bank, and pay back an agreed amount every month.

C You apply to the local authority (council) or housing association. People who are most in need are given housing first. Some people may not be offered a home. Others have to wait for a long time.

Groups of people

1. A student
2. A family with two adults earning a regular wage
3. A family on a low income
4. A young, single professional person
5. An elderly person on a low income
6. A migrant newly arrived in this country
7. A young couple who do not have any savings

Tenure	How it works (A, B or C)	Groups of people most likely to have this type of housing tenure (there is more than one answer for some boxes)
Owner occupation		
Renting from a private landlord		
Renting from a social landlord		

Figure A Different types of housing tenure

2 Use the information in Figure 2 on page 2 to complete the sentences below by underlining the correct answer.

In 1981 *more / fewer* people owned a house than in 2007. Tenants renting from

a social landlord *increased / decreased* from *32 per cent / 57 per cent* in 1981 to

70 per cent / 18 per cent in 2007. In 2007 there were slightly *more / fewer* people

renting from a private landlord than in 1981.

3 Study Figure 3 on page 3. It gives advantages and disadvantages of each type of housing tenure, but they are jumbled up.

   a) Decide whether each statement in the table below is an advantage or disadvantage.

   i) Colour the advantages green.   **ii)** Colour the disadvantages blue.

   b) Work in pairs to decide which type of housing tenure is being described by each statement. Place the number on the correct part of the Venn diagram in Figure B.

1	Someone else pays for repairs to your home.
2	You have to have a lot of savings before you can borrow the rest of the money for a mortgage.
3	What you pay each month is fair and affordable.
4	When the mortgage is paid, the value of the home is yours.
5	Your home could be repossessed if you miss payments.
6	You can move at short notice.
7	A very wide variety of properties is available at all sorts of prices.
8	You can choose to extend your home (with planning permission).
9	You have very little choice about which house becomes your home.
10	You might wait a long time to get repairs done if you have a bad landlord.

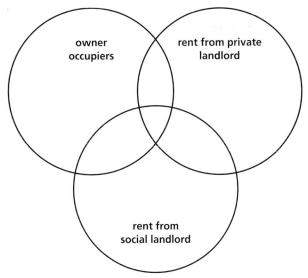

Figure B The advantages and disadvantages of each housing tenure

4 Use www.rightmove.co.uk or your local property paper to:

   a) find the different costs of renting or buying property in your area

   b) compare costs of housing between an urban and rural area.

Review what you have learned

I can:

- describe three different types of housing tenure ☐
- give one advantage of each type of housing tenure ☐
- give one disadvantage of each type of housing tenure. ☐

How does the urban environment affect quality of life?

In these activities you will:

■ consider how features of the urban environment can affect your quality of life.

See Student's Book pages 4–5

1 Study Figure 6 on page 4. Complete the table below.

   a) Decide if the feature will have a **positive** or **negative** effect on quality of life and add a tick to the correct column (some will have both a positive and negative effect).

   b) Describe how the feature might affect people. One has been done for you. Notice how the word **so** is used to add elaboration to the answer.

Feature of the environment that is close to home	Pos.	Neg.	How it affects quality of life
On a busy main road	✓		Good access to public transport **so** … people can get to shops, jobs and entertainment quickly and easily.
		✓	Difficult to cross the road **so** … parents may be worried about their young children.
Under the flight path of an airport		✓	The aircraft are noisy **so** … it could keep families awake
Next to empty buildings that have been burned or vandalised		✓	He /she might be worried about crime
Some small shops within walking distance of your house	✓		Can easily get food/confectionary
School near to your home with a good reputation	✓		families will have a good school within their catchment area to send their children to.
A pub and some takeaways nearby	✓		A nice place to socialize
		✓	could encourage unhealthy eating
		✓	could be violence at pub
Lots of open green spaces and woodland nearby			
A very popular gym and sports centre nearby			

2 Study Figure 7 on page 4. It shows how the negative effects of a pub on local residents reduce with distance. Distance matters when it comes to quality of life!

Describe how quality of life might be affected by distance from the following urban features. The effects could be good or bad. One has been done for you.

a) An Accident and Emergency (A&E) hospital.

> Living in the countryside, many miles from A&E, could be a disadvantage if you had an accident because it could take a long time to get treated. However, living very close to an A&E could also be a disadvantage because the noise from emergency vehicles could disturb you all day and night.

b) A Premier League football ground.

As there are often fights at football this could have a bad influence on children living nearby as it could encourage violence. It will also be very noisy and keep people awake.

c) A skate park.

A skatepark is a place to sosialise with friends. However it could encourage crime.

d) A takeaway.

This can encourage unhealthy eating, however it can also provide an easy access of getting food if person is busy.

Review what you have learned

I can:

- describe how three features of the urban environment can have positive and negative effects on quality of life ☐

- explain why distance from an urban feature matters to quality of life. ☐

What is it like living in the inner city of Cardiff?

In these activities you will:

■ think about how deprivation is measured;

■ describe patterns of deprivation from a shaded (choropleth) map.

See Student's Book pages 10–11

1 Study page 10 and the key words below. Tick (✓) the correct definition for each term.

a) What is **standard of living**?

☐ A measure of the relative wealth of individuals or families

☑ A measure of happiness and contentment for individuals

☐ A measure of how much money a person earns in a year

b) What does it mean if a person is living in **poverty**?

☐ Not having enough money for a place to live

☐ Having a very low income

☐ Having very poor health

c) What is **deprivation**?

☐ Lacking some basic needs of life, such as education, clean water, enough food or equality

☐ Having a very low income

☐ How people feel when they don't have enough money

2 Study Figure 20 on page 10 which shows the different things that the Welsh Government uses when measuring deprivation. Complete the sentences below to show how these factors can affect a person's life. One has been done for you.

a) Income – If you have a low income … you may find it difficult to pay the rent, electricity bills **and** buy food for your children, so you are faced with very difficult choices.

b) Education, skills and training – If you have few qualifications or lack training

It will be difficult to get a job therefore you will not have a stable income.

c) Access to services – If you do not live near services that you need, for example doctors or a school

If you don't live near a doctor it could mean you will have slow healthcare service.

d) Community safety – If the area you live in has a lot of crime

e) Housing – If your house is too small for your family or it has problems like damp

3 Study Figure 21 on page 10. It shows deprivation in Riverside, part of the inner city of Cardiff. The dark red areas are the most deprived (see the key above Figure 21). You are going to draw your own shaded (choropleth) map of Grangetown, another part of inner city Cardiff.

Use Figure 23 on page 10 to colour Figure A below to create your deprivation map of Grangetown. Remember to colour your key.

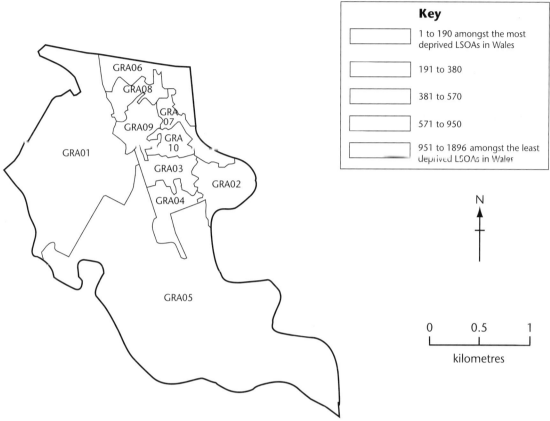

Key

	1 to 190 amongst the most deprived LSOAs in Wales
	191 to 380
	381 to 570
	571 to 950
	951 to 1896 amongst the least deprived LSOAs in Wales

N

0   0.5   1
kilometres

Figure A Map showing deprivation in Grangetown, Cardiff

✎ **4** When you have coloured the map, describe the pattern of deprivation in Grangetown.

5 Use Figures 24 and 25 on page 11 to complete the following sentences. Fill in the gaps and underline the correct answer. One has been done for you.

a) The highest percentage of Black ethnic population is in the ward of … Butetown … which is **south-west** / <u>**south-east**</u> of the CBD.

b) The highest percentage of Asian ethnic population is in the ward of

.... which is **west** / **east** of the CBD.

c) The highest percentage of mixed ethnic groups is in the ward of

.... which is **south-west** / **south-east** of the CBD.

Review what you have learned

I can:

- present information on a shaded (choropleth) map ☐

- describe three facts about life in the inner city of Cardiff. ☐

What is it like living in Nairobi?

In these activities you will:

See Student's Book pages 12–15

- describe how quality of life of Nairobi's poorest residents is affected by their environment;
- consider how informal housing could be improved.

1 Match the following key words to their definitions in the table below.

a) Informal housing   **b)** Insecurity of tenure   **c)** Informal jobs   **d)** Sanitation

Key word	Definition
	The safe disposal and treatment of sewage and waste water
	When householders have no legal right to be in their home and could be evicted at any time
	An area of housing where the householders have no legal right to the land
	Work that does not have set hours or set wages

2 Study Figure 27 on page 12.

a) Add **four** labels to Figure A using the ideas in the box below.

water   roads / pavements   building materials   size of homes   housing density

b) Add detail to each label to show how people are affected by this environment. One has been done for you.

Housing is very high density so fires and disease will spread easily.

Figure A Sketch of informal housing in Kibera

3 Study Figures 30 and 31 on pages 14–15. They show information about informal housing in Kibera.

a) Complete the table below to show how living in this area can affect people's quality of life.

Problem for residents living in this area	Effect on quality of life
Housing is made of scrap material	so the houses sometimes collapse causing injuries.
Alleyways between the huts do not have street lighting	
People do not pay council tax and their views are often ignored by the local authority	
The residents do not own the land and could be thrown out of their homes at any time by the police	
There is a river running through the settlement which is contaminated with sewage and other waste	
HIV infection rates are high	
Homes do not have piped water or sewers	
The area is low lying and likely to flood when it rains	

b) Choose **one** of the problems in the table above. Suggest how local residents could make an improvement.

c) Choose **two** more problems. Suggest how the local authority could make an improvement.

4 Use the internet to research other factors that affect quality of life in Kibera.

Review what you have learned

I can:
- use key terms to do with formal and informal housing ☐
- give five features of Kibera that would affect quality of life ☐
- describe three ways that Kibera could be improved. ☐

Introduction to shops and services

In these activities you will:

- consider why shops that sell different types of goods tend to be located in different parts of a city.

See Student's Book pages 19–22

1 Match the following key words to their definitions in the table below.

a) Convenience goods   **d)** Comparison goods   **f)** Central Business District (CBD)

b) Catchment area   **e)** Hierarchy   **g)** Suburbs

c) Threshold population

Key word	Definition
	Putting things in order of size
	The minimum number of customers needed by a shop
	Less expensive items that customers buy often
	The centre of an urban area where shops are found
	More expensive items that customers buy less often
	The area from which a shop gets its customers
	Neighbourhoods on the outskirts of an urban area

2 a) Choose examples of comparison and convenience goods from the box below and write them under the correct heading in Figure A.

bread	sofa	television	car	milk
fridge	newspapers and magazines		fruit and vegetables	

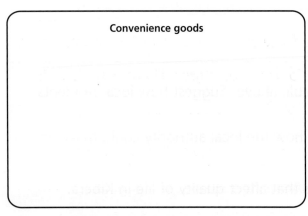

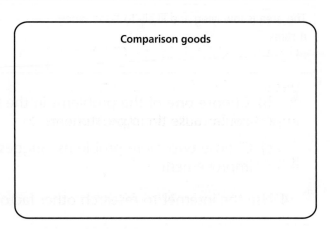

Figure A Examples of convenience and comparison goods

b) Now add some examples of your own to Figure A. Try to think of at least five examples.

3 Study Figure 2 on page 19.

a) Complete Figure B opposite to show retail (shopping) hierarchy by adding real examples from the area where you live.

b) Complete the caption for Figure B by adding the name of your town/city.

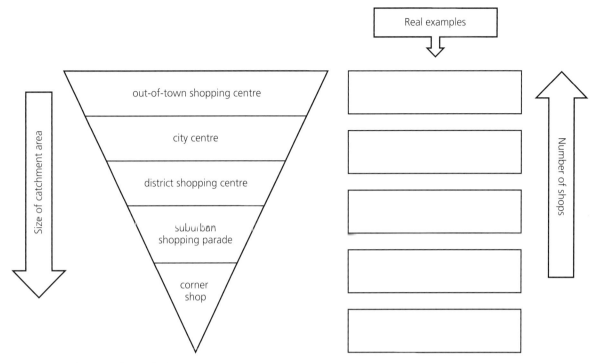

Figure B A shopping hierarchy in ....

4 Study Figure 4 on page 20 which is a photo of a large superstore in Cardiff. The location of this store is shown on Figure 9 on page 22. Use Figure 9 on page 22 and your own knowledge to complete the sentences below to explain why this is an ideal site for a large superstore.

A large superstore is located in grid square .... This is an ideal site for such a

large building because the superstore needs lots of land for ....

It is located on the edge of the city, ... km from the CBD (measure from

Figure 6, which is in the CBD). It is close to a large area of housing which is important

because a lot of the .... for the superstore will live here. It is also

important because the superstore needs a lot of ....

It is close to a main road called the .... which is important because the

superstore needs good access for .... and ....

Review what you have learned
I can:
- use key terms to do with retail hierarchies ☐
- give five examples each of convenience and comparison goods ☐
- give three reasons why superstores like to be located on the edge of large urban areas. ☐

Distribution of services

In these activities you will:

- consider the way in which services are distributed;
- describe the distribution of services in a case study of Barcelona.

See Student's Book pages 28–32

Case study: Distribution of services in Barcelona

1 Study the **four** distribution patterns (regular, random, clustered, linear) on page 29. Use this diagram, and your own knowledge, to complete Figure A below.

Pattern	Name	Examples of services with this distribution pattern
a)	Regular	
b)		Open spaces / parks in a city
c)	Clustered	
d)		Motorway services

Figure A Distribution patterns

2 Study Figure 27 on page 30 which shows the distribution of mosques in Barcelona. Complete the sentences below by underlining the correct answer.

The mosques in the Ciutat Vella area of Barcelona are distributed in a **linear / clustered** pattern. They are mainly located around the **central / suburban** area of the city.

They are located here because this is the largest area of Muslim migrants from

Morocco / Mexico and Pakistan.

The people living in the **north-west / north-east** areas of Barcelona do not have good access to mosques.

3 Study Figure 32 on page 32 which shows the distribution of badminton courts in Barcelona. Complete the sentences below using words from the box below.

clustered	linear	regular	random	Ciutat Vella
Sarria-Sant Gervasi	north	south	east	north-west
south-west	lowest	highest	central suburban	

Badminton courts in Barcelona are distributed in a .... pattern.

People living in the .... areas of Barcelona have the best access to

badminton courts. This is because people have to pay to use the badminton courts and

most people living in this area have the .... incomes in Barcelona.

People living in the .... areas of Barcelona do not have good

access to badminton courts. This is because most people living in these areas have the

.... incomes in Barcelona.

4 Complete the sentences below.

Conclusion: Mosques in Barcelona have a .... pattern.

This is because ....

....

Conclusion: Badminton courts in Barcelona have a .... pattern.

However, the poorest districts of Barcelona do not have any badminton courts. This is

because ....

....

Review what you have learned
I can:
- use terms that describe distribution patterns with confidence ☐
- use Barcelona as a case study to describe the distribution of one type of service ☐
- give two reasons why access to services varies. ☐

How are planners tackling urban problems in Barcelona?

See Student's Book pages 30–33, 38–39

In these activities you will:

■ develop a case study of the inner urban area of Barcelona

■ examine how El Raval was improved through a process of **gentrification**.

1 Study pages 30 to 33. Use information from these pages to complete the following sentences by underlining the correct answers.

Barcelona's ethnic groups mainly live in the **inner / outer** urban areas of Barcelona. In El Raval **27.6 per cent / 6 per cent** of the population is made up of foreign migrants to the city. This is **lower / higher** than the average for the whole city which is 7.2 per cent.

El Raval is an area in the old city centre (Ciutat Vella) and has **ten / seven / three** of the sixteen mosques in Barcelona so this is one reason why Muslim migrants choose to live in this area. El Raval has other features that make it popular with migrants from Pakistan and **Poland / Morocco / Spain** including halal butchers, shops with internet and global telephone connections and Asian video stores.

The housing in the area of El Raval is **high / low** density. The area of El Raval has the second-lowest **housing density / life expectancy** in Barcelona. The number of people with malaria, AIDS and TB is **higher / lower** than in Barcelona as a whole.

2 Study Figure 12 on page 39. Label the photo below with three problems that needed to be addressed by planners.

Figure A Housing in El Raval

Gentrification in Barcelona

Planners in Barcelona have tried to improve the overcrowded areas of the city such as El Raval. El Raval is now becoming a more popular neighbourhood for young families to live in. This process is known as **gentrification**. Study the information on pages 38 and 39 before answering the following questions.

3 Study the statements in the boxes below. Sort the statements into two types:

- **problems** that planners needed to solve to improve the city
- **solutions** that the planners have used.

Colour the problems in red and the solutions in green.

Planners have demolished some of the old apartment blocks in El Raval so the population density is now lower.	Public transport has been improved. It is harder for car owners to drive around the city so it is safer to walk around.
Drug dealing and prostitution were common in El Raval so tourists were warned not to visit the area.	The run-down, industrial areas around the port of Barcelona put people off visiting the city.
New museums and art galleries have been opened so people have more leisure opportunities.	New parks and gardens have been created so there are places to relax and safe places for children to play.
When people made a noise late at night (for example, shouting or using motorbikes) the residents of El Raval could not sleep.	The city authorities started to fine people on the spot for making too much noise so there is a more peaceful environment.
People are fined for vandalism such as graffiti so that the local residents have pride in the area and it attracts visitors.	The local authority listened to the views of local residents and provided them with what they wanted.
The streets of El Raval were narrow and congested. It was difficult for people to get to work and for local businesses to run efficiently.	In 1980, 4 per cent of people in Barcelona lived in homes that were unfit to live in and many more people lived in overcrowded conditions.

 4 Study the statements in the boxes above. Imagine you are a planner.

    a) Rank the problems starting with the one that needs solving first. Explain why you would tackle this problem.

    b) Choose the solution to this problem. Say how successful you think it has been.

Review what you have learned

I can:

- describe three problems faced by planners in El Raval   ☐
- describe how these three problems were solved.   ☐

Investigating patterns of migration in South Africa

See Student's Book pages 40–43

In these activities you will:

- explain why people are moving from the countryside (**rural** areas) to cities (**urban** areas);
- consider the impacts of migration on both urban and rural areas.

1 Match the following key words to their definitions in the table below.

a) Migration   d) Net migration   g) Rural   j) Brain drain

b) Economic migrant   e) Push factors   h) Poverty line   k) Remittances

c) Natural population change   f) Pull factors   i) Urban   l) Circular migration

Key word	Definition
	When people move from living in one place to live in another
	Reasons a person moves to a place
	The difference between the birth and death rates
	Built up areas; towns and cities
	The movement and return of people between rural and urban areas
	The difference between the number of people moving into an area and the number of people moving out of an area
	A person who moves to live somewhere else to earn money
	When people live below a level of income and are said to be poor
	Reasons a person moves away from a place
	Money sent by migrant workers to support their families who have remained at home
	The countryside
	When an area loses highly qualified workers due to emigration

2 Limpopo is South Africa's most rural province. Many people move from here to Guateng which is the neighbouring province. We need to investigate why this is.

a) Study Figure 16 on page 40. Use the information from this map and other information on pages 40–43 to complete the fact boxes in Figures A, B and C.

The province of Gauteng has an urban population of .... per cent.	The province of Limpopo has an urban population of .... per cent.
Gauteng has three cities of more than 1 million including	The largest city in Limpopo has a population of ....
The number of people in Gauteng with no schooling is	The number of people in Limpopo with no schooling is ....

Figure A Comparing life in Gauteng to Limpopo

<table>
<tr><td>

Pull factors

Housing in Gauteng is ....

....

....

</td><td>

Push factors

Housing in Limpopo is ....

....

....

</td></tr>
<tr><td>

Income in Gauteng is ....

....

....

</td><td>

Income in Limpopo is ....

....

....

</td></tr>
<tr><td>

The percentage of people living below the poverty line in Gauteng is lower than that of Limpopo at ....

</td><td>

The percentage of people living below the poverty line in Limpopo is ....

</td></tr>
</table>

Figure B Why are people moving from Limpopo to Gauteng?

<table>
<tr><td>

Negative impacts of the rural to urban migration on Gauteng include ....

....

....

....

....

</td><td>

Negative impacts of the rural to urban migration on Limpopo include ....

....

....

....

....

</td></tr>
<tr><td>

Positive impacts of the rural to urban migration on Gauteng include ....

....

....

....

....

</td><td>

Positive impacts of the rural to urban migration on Limpopo include ....

....

....

....

....

</td></tr>
</table>

Figure C What are the impacts of migration? (Read pages 42–43.)

Review what you have learned

I can:

- describe three push and three pull factors ☐
- use South Africa as a case study of migration, giving three facts. ☐

Is the UK suffering a housing crisis?

See Student's Book pages 48–49

In these activities you will:

- think about where new housing should be built;
- describe the features that make BedZED a sustainable community.

1 Study page 48 and the key words below. Complete each sentence.

a) **Urban sprawl** is when the growth of suburbs is ....

b) **Green belts** are wide zones around major UK cities in which development is

....

c) **Greenfield sites** have never ....

d) **Brownfield sites** have been built on before. The old buildings may be unused or

....

e) One advantage of building on brownfield sites is that ....

....

2 Planners are worried that there is not enough housing in the UK to meet people's needs.

a) Read the information on page 48 and 49.

b) Match up the numbers in the box to the statements in Figure A.

223,000	3 million	240,000	13%	300,000–399,000
11 million	10%	13 million	6.7%	

The number of people in 2003 in the UK who were aged over 65:	The number of extra homes which need to be built between 2007 and 2020:	The expected growth rate of the East of England:
The number of new homes the government wants to see built every year by 2016:	The number of new homes needed every year to meet demand:	The area of England currently occupied by green belts:
The number of over 65s expected to be living in the UK by 2026:	The expected growth rate of the UK population:	The number of new homes needed to be built by 2026 in the West Midlands:

Figure A The UK's housing in numbers

Case study: BedZED – a sustainable community

Key word: Something is **sustainable** when it meets people's needs now and in the future.

Something is **socially sustainable** when it provides benefits for families, health, education and leisure.	Something is **environmentally sustainable** if it conserves air quality, habitats and wildlife.	Something is **economically sustainable** when it creates jobs, income and spending.

1 Below are features of the BedZED sustainable community.

   a) Colour socially sustainable features in yellow.

   b) Colour economically sustainable features in blue.

   c) Colour environmentally sustainable features in green.

Some statements may be sustainable in more than one way. You could choose to colour the statement in more than one colour.

A BedZED uses solar energy and woodchips to heat the homes and provide power.	**D** There is a crèche, youth group and community centre. These provide facilities for people of all ages.	**G** Roof gardens soak up rainwater so less flows into storm drains.
B BedZED is a carbon-neutral development – the homes do not add any extra carbon dioxide emissions into the atmosphere.	**E** There is a car pool for residents to reduce the number of car journeys.	**H** The buildings are very well insulated which conserves heat energy in the homes.
C There is a mix of tenures including fifteen homes at affordable rent for social housing.	**F** Where possible, the buildings have been built from natural, recycled or reclaimed materials.	**I** There are large windows which face south to collect heat energy from the Sun.

 2 Choose **three** statements (from B–I). Explain why each is sustainable. One has been done for you.

A BedZED uses solar energy and woodchips to heat the homes and provide power. This is environmentally sustainable because less fossil fuel will be burned so BedZED makes a smaller contribution to climate change.

Review what you have learned

I can:

■ give the differences between a brownfield site and a greenfield site ☐

■ describe three features that make BedZED sustainable. ☐

A planning issue: where to locate an airport?

See Student's Book pages 60–61

In these activities you will see that:

- people have conflicting views over whether the UK needs a new airport;
- when planners make decisions, they consider different points of view.

1 Study Figure 26 on page 61 and the statements in the boxes below.

   a) Decide whether each statement is **for** or **against** the expansion of airports.

   b) Decide whether the statement is making a **social** argument, an **economic** argument or an **environmental** argument.

	For (✓) or against (✗)	Social Economic Environmental
A Expanding airports will create new jobs in construction. There will also be new jobs at the new airports.		
B Some homes will be bulldozed to make space for new runways. These home owners will have to move from their community.		
C The expansion of airports is good for the UK economy because it means more foreign visitors.		
D Carbon dioxide released from aircraft is contributing to climate change.		
E Noise from aircraft landing and taking off is stressful for home-owners who live under the flight path. It can reduce house prices.		
F Expanding UK airports would mean a loss of farmland which could mean more reliance on importing food in the future.		
G Technology is being developed to make aircraft cleaner and more efficient. This will reduce their impact on climate change.		
H Passengers could be charged higher taxes when using air travel to try to reduce the number of people flying.		
I Some air companies encourage passengers to pay a charge which is used to plant trees. This helps to offset the impact of aircraft on the atmosphere.		

2 Study Figure 25 on page 60. Name one group who might be:

a) in favour of a new runway at Heathrow: ....

Explain why they have this view. ....

....

b) against a new runway at Heathrow: ....

Explain why they have this view. ....

....

c) against a new airport at Cliffe: ....

Explain why they have this view. ....

....

3 How can the problem be solved? Use information from pages 60 and 61 to complete the following table. You could also research the issue on the internet.

A Build a new runway at Heathrow	Positive impacts of this decision	
	Negative impacts of this decision	
B Build a brand-new airport at Cliffe in the Thames Estuary	Positive impacts of this decision	
	Negative impacts of this decision	

4 Decide which of these two alternatives you think is the best option for the UK. In your answer you should include:

- which option you think is best
- why you think it is the best option (give at least two reasons)
- how you think the negative impacts of your decision could be reduced.

Review what you have learned

I can:

- name two different groups of people who have strong opinions about this issue ☐
- summarise the main argument used by each of these groups. ☐

Rural housing issues

In these activities you will:

■ examine the reasons for the shortage of homes in the countryside;
■ consider how village life is changing.

See Student's Book pages 63–67, 76

1 Read page 63. Complete the following definitions with a key term:

a) Rural regions that are close to or well connected to cities by roads are described

as being ....

b) Many people are moving from cities into accessible rural areas such as Kent. This

process is known as ....

c) Rural regions that are a long way from cities or difficult to get to are described as

being ....

d) Some people who live in remote rural regions are leaving the countryside. This

process is known as .... (Read page 76.) An example of a region

like this is .... in the country of ....

2 Study Figure 3 on page 64.

a) A lot of people now **telework** from homes in the countryside. Give **three** changes that have made it possible for more people to live and work in the countryside. One has been started for you.

i) More powerful computers so ....

....

ii) ....

....

iii) ....

....

b) Give **two** changes that make it possible to easily visit the countryside for leisure activities.

i) ....

ii) ....

3 The process of counter-urbanisation means there are now social differences between rural and urban regions in the UK. In this activity you will examine differences in population structure and occupation.

a) Study Figure 5 on page 65. Complete the following table. Some answers have been completed for you.

Population	Shrewsbury (urban)	connective	Clun (rural)
Aged 60–74	14%	whereas	22% are 60–74 which is 8% higher.
Aged 20–29			
Aged 10–19	14%		

b) Complete the following conclusion about population structure.

There are more .... people in rural Shropshire than in

urban areas. There are a lot fewer people aged ....

in rural areas, perhaps because they have left to look for work.

c) Use Figure 6 on page 65 to complete the following conclusion about occupation:

There are a lot more .... people in rural Shropshire

than in urban areas. However, there are slightly fewer highly-skilled occupations such

as ....

4 Why is there a shortage of homes in rural areas of the UK? Study Figure 7 on page 66 and use the information to join the heads and tails below.

Demand from second-home owners increases …
There are few council houses left in rural areas because of the right-to-buy schemes introduced in the 1980s …
Very few houses are built in rural areas because planners do not want to build houses on greenfield or greenbelt sites …
An increasing number of people are retiring to rural areas …
More people own cars and transport is more efficient …

… because people are living longer and there are more affluent older people who can afford to move wherever they want.
… so more people can commute to work from rural areas to their job in the city or town.
… so the supply of housing in rural areas is small.
… so the price of rural housing increases.
… so there is not enough social housing.

Review what you have learned

I can:

- give three reasons why people are able to telework ☐
- describe three differences between urban and rural populations ☐
- give three reasons why there is a shortage of homes in the countryside. ☐

Managing leisure use at Ynyslas

In these activities you will:

- describe the location of Ynyslas
- describe how visitors have damaged the ecosystem here
- say how successful the management strategies here have been.

See Student's Book pages 70–71

Case study: Ynyslas National Nature Reserve

1 Use Figure A to describe the location of Ynyslas National Nature Reserve by underlining the correct answers.

Ynyslas is located in **west** /**east** / **south** Wales. It is

- north of the town of **Conwy / Aberystwyth / Wrexham**

- **100 / 120 / 150 km** from Cardiff

- on the coast next to **Cardigan Bay / Bristol Channel**

- located south of **Pembrokeshire / Snowdonia / Brecon Beacons** national park.

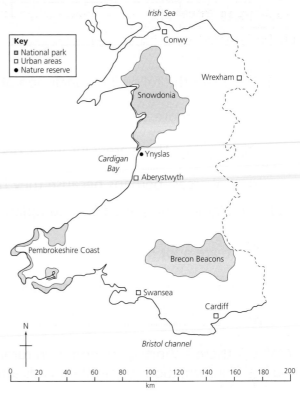

Figure A The location of Ynyslas National Nature Reserve

2 Human activities can cause erosion of sand dunes. Read the information at the top of page 70 and complete the diagram below.

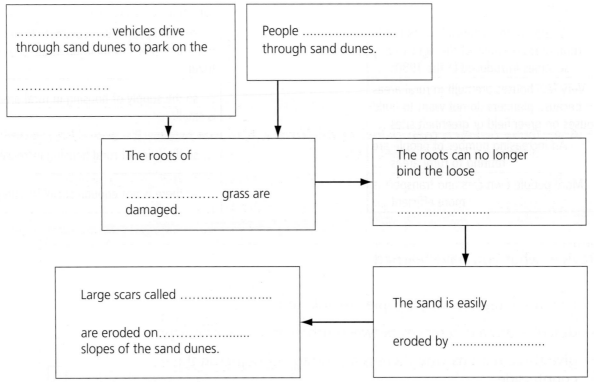

.... vehicles drive through sand dunes to park on the

....

People .... through sand dunes.

The roots of

.... grass are damaged.

The roots can no longer bind the loose

....

Large scars called ....

are eroded on........................ slopes of the sand dunes.

The sand is easily

eroded by ....

Figure B The process of sand dune erosion

3 Wardens at Ynyslas have introduced a number of strategies to try to manage the damage caused by human activity at the National Nature Reserve.

a) Read the information in Figure 16 on page 70 and 71 about what the wardens have done.

b) Complete the table below to evaluate the strategies. One has been done for you.

Damage or threat	How it is being managed	Evaluation of strategy
1. Driving vehicles through the dunes causes erosion	Put posts into the beach	Successful because cars cannot be driven onto the beach so plants grow and prevent further wind erosion
2. Visitors trample through the sand dunes		
3. Litter		
4. Visitors disturb the songbirds nesting on the ground		
5. Dog fouling		

✎ 4 a) Draw a sketch map below of the Ynyslas National Nature Reserve. Use Figure 16 on pages 70–71 to help you.

b) Add numbers from the table above to show where there are problems.

c) Add labels to show how these problems are being managed.

Review what you have learned

I can:

■ describe a location using a compass point and scale line ☐

■ describe three different ways that visitors cause damage to the dunes at Ynyslas ☐

■ describe three management strategies and say how successful they have been. ☐

How do leisure activities affect rural parts of Iceland?

See Student's Book pages 72–77

In these activities you will:

- use a map to find evidence to support an argument;
- describe the benefits of tourism for the economy of rural Iceland.

1 a) Many people visit the wild landscapes of Iceland. Study the photos on pages 74 and 140. Imagine you are there. In the table below, place a cross in one box on each row to show how you feel about Gulfoss (the waterfall).

magical						ordinary
familiar						alien
awe-inspiring						boring
wild						tamed
roaring						tranquil

Read about bi-polar surveys on page 13 of the Student's Book

 b) Work in pairs to discuss the results of the bi-polar table above. How could you use this technique to assess the tourist qualities of a landscape?

2 Geysir and Gullfoss are popular tourist attractions. Study Figure 20 on page 73. Gullfoss is in the top right corner of the map (in grid 0928).

a) Complete the following sentences to describe the location of Geysir by underlining the correct answer.

Geysir is **west / east / south-east** of Gullfoss and about **5 / 10 / 15** km by road

from the waterfall. Many tourists stay in Selfoss which is about **45 / 65 / 85** km

away to the **south-east / south-west / north-east**.

b) Trekking, horse riding, camping, climbing and cycling are all popular leisure activities in this part of Iceland. The symbols in blue in Figure 20 on page 73 are for leisure facilities. A key for them is given in Figure A below.

 Camping Petrol station Picnic Guest house Golf Swimming

Figure A Symbols for tourist/leisure facilities in Figure 20 on page 73

Match the following grid squares to the correct combination of facilities. One has been done for you.

0627   0726   0624   0118   0322

Grid ref	Tourist / leisure facilities
0624	Swimming, petrol station
	Camping, swimming, petrol station, golf
	Camping, swimming, petrol station, golf, hotel or guest house
	Picnic, camping
	Swimming, camping, petrol station

✎ **c)** Use the photographs and map on pages 73–74 to write a short advert to attract tourists to visit Geysir and Gullfoss.

3 Tourism and leisure activities create a lot of benefits in the economy of the rural area.

a) Study page 74 and Figure B below, which shows the effect of a **positive multiplier** on the area around Gullfoss.

b) Complete the blank spaces in Figure B by adding words from boxes 1 and 2 below.

c) Use **two** colours to shade the boxes in Figure B to show the cause and effects of tourism.

Box 1

roads, schools and hospitals

car hire companies and coach companies

shops and restaurants

banks and building societies

waiters, cleaners and hotel receptionists

Box 2

more

less

the same

You will need to use words from this box more than once.

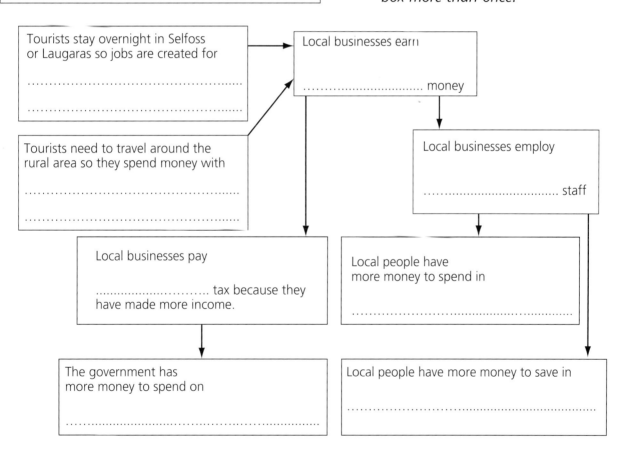

Figure B The positive multiplier effect in rural Iceland

Review what you have learned

I can:

- describe a location using a scale line and compass ☐
- find evidence (of leisure activities) on a detailed map ☐
- describe three benefits of tourism for rural Iceland. ☐

Physical Processes and Relationships between People and Environments

Continental and maritime climates

In these activities you will:

■ investigate winter temperature patterns in Europe;

■ discover the influence of the Atlantic Ocean on Europe's climate.

See Student's Book pages 80–85

The ocean does not get as cold as the earth during winter. The Atlantic Ocean acts a bit like a hot water bottle during the winter and warms up the surrounding areas! It gives western Europe a winter that is wet and warm. This is a **maritime** climate. Eastern Europe, which is further from the ocean, is much colder in winter. It has a **continental** climate.

1 a) Complete this prediction by underlining the correct words.

I expect that winter temperatures in western Europe will be **warmer** / **the same** /

colder than in eastern Europe. I also expect temperatures to get **warmer** / **colder** as

you travel from the Mediterranean towards the Arctic. The coldest part of Europe in

winter will be the **south-west** / **east** / **north-east**. The warmest part will be the

north-west / **south-west** / **south-east**.

b) Plot the temperatures in Figure A opposite onto Figure B. Use an atlas or the internet to find each location.

c) Add colour to your map by shading each shape made by the lines of latitude and longitude. Use 'warm' colours like orange for the temperatures above zero. Use 'cold' colours like shades of blue for temperatures below zero.

d) Were the predictions you made at the start of this enquiry correct? **Yes / No**

✎ **e)** Compare the temperatures in Iceland to those in Finland and Russia at the same latitude. Explain this difference in temperature.

2 Why is it colder in Arctic Europe than in the Mediterranean? Study Figure 2 on page 80. Underline the correct words in the following passage.

Location	Temp °C
Lisbon	8
Rome	5
Bordeaux	2
Reykjavik	−2
Berlin	−3
Ankara	−4
Warsaw	−6
Oslo	−7
Bucharest	−7
Helsinki	−9
Kiev	−10
St Petersburg	−13

Figure A Average minimum January temperature °C

In the northernmost parts of Europe, the Sun's energy

hits the ground at a **low angle** / **right angle**, so winter

temperatures are very **low** / **high** and the summer season is **short** / **long**. The Sun is

higher overhead in southern Europe, so winter temperatures here are **colder** / **warmer**

and summers are **shorter** / **longer** than in the Arctic.

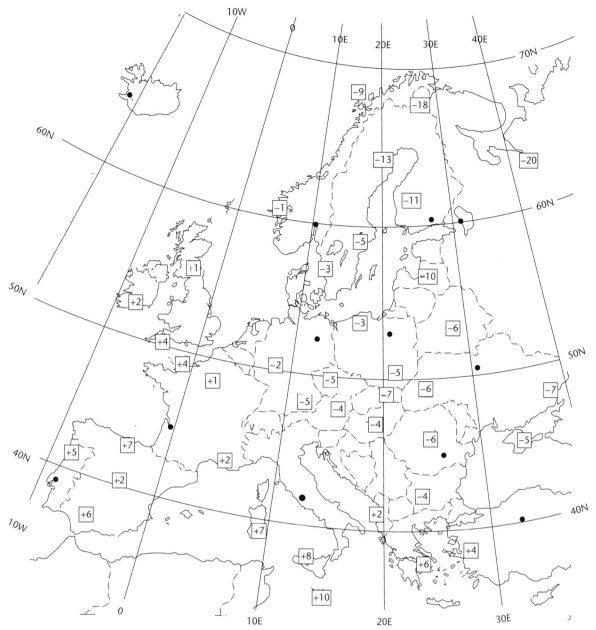

Figure B Average minimum January temperatures across Europe °C

Review what you have learned

I can:

- use an atlas to find the location of cities ☐

- describe the pattern of winter temperatures across Europe ☐

- explain why western Europe has a warmer climate than eastern Europe in winter. ☐

What is the tropical climate like?

In these activities you will:

- practise drawing climate graphs;
- describe the tropical climate;
- explain why it rains so much in the tropics.

See Student's Book pages 81, 88–89

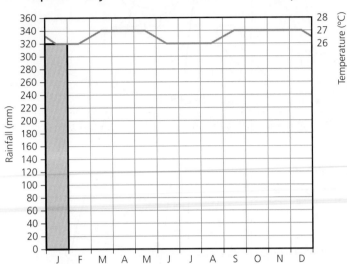

Figure A Climate chart for Belem, Brazil

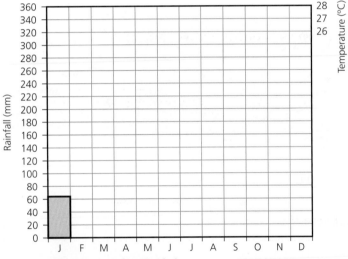

Figure B Climate chart for Trinidad

1 Use Figure 22 on page 89 to complete the two climate charts in Figures A and B. The temperature line has already been completed for Figure A.

2 a) Read the text 'Describing a climate graph' on page 81.

✎ **b)** Describe **one** similarity and **one** difference between Figures A and B.

c) Complete this conclusion:

In a tropical climate, the temperature in every month is ....

The total amount of rainfall can vary from one part of the tropics to another, but

several months have ....

It rains more in Belem than in Trinidad because Belem is nearer to the ....

3 Why does it rain so much in the tropics? Study Figures 19 and 20 on page 88. Use them to complete the diagram below.

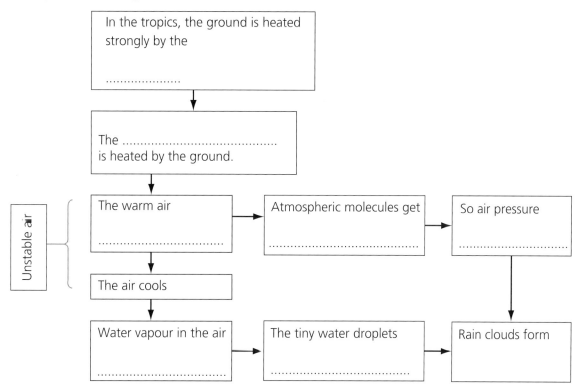

In the tropics, the ground is heated strongly by the

....

The ....
is heated by the ground.

Unstable air

The warm air

....

Atmospheric molecules get

....

So air pressure

....

The air cools

Water vapour in the air

....

The tiny water droplets

....

Rain clouds form

4 Show you know what the tropical climate is like. Spot the odd one out.

a) In each row, circle the odd one out.

					Common theme
1.	Cold winters	Hot summers	Heavy rainfall	High humidity	
2.	Drought	High pressure	Cloudless skies	Strong wind	
3.	Strong wind	Heavy rainfall	Cloudless skies	Low pressure	
4.	Trinidad	Belem, Brazil	Ghana	Iceland	
5.	Unstable air	High pressure	Condensation	Rain clouds	

b) For each row, state what the three remaining words have in common. Write your answer in the final column of the table.

Review what you have learned

I can:
- draw and describe a climate graph ☐
- explain why it rains so much in the tropics. ☐

Low pressure systems

In these activities you will:

- practise reading from a weather map (synoptic chart);
- develop a case study of a tropical cyclone.

See Student's
Book pages
92–93 and 96–97

1 Study Figure 26 on page 92. It shows low pressure (a depression) over Iceland. Show you understand this weather map by adding the following details to Figure A.

a) Colour the wedge of warm air in red and the area of cold air in blue.

b) Label the 1000mb and 1016mb isobars.

c) Add the letter L to the centre of the low pressure.

d) Label one place on the map where you expect wind speeds are strong.

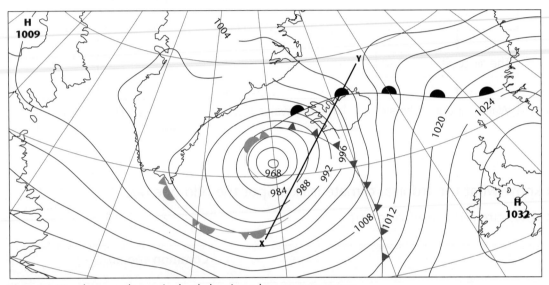

Figure A Weather map (synoptic chart) showing a low pressure system

2 Complete Figure B, which is a cross section (X–Y) through the depression in Figure A.

a) Colour the warm sector in red and the cold sector in blue.

b) Add labels a)–h) to Figure B from the box below:

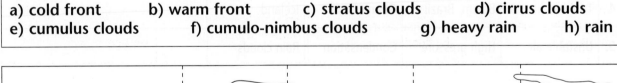

a) cold front	b) warm front	c) stratus clouds	d) cirrus clouds
e) cumulus clouds	f) cumulo-nimbus clouds	g) heavy rain	h) rain

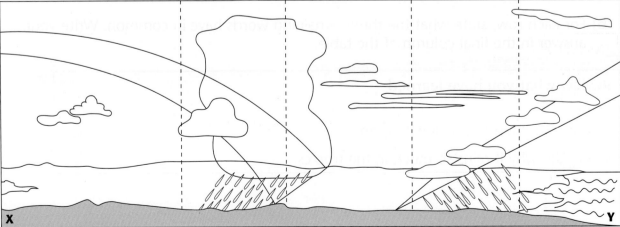

Figure B Cross-section X–Y through the depression on Figure A

Case study: Cyclone Nargis

3 Study Figure 34 on page 96. Describe the track of Cyclone Nargis by underlining the correct answers in the following passage.

Cyclone Nargis started as a **tropical depression / tropical storm / hurricane** in the Indian Ocean on 29 April 2008. It travelled in a **south-westerly / north-westerly / south-easterly** direction until 30 April. It then changed direction and moved towards **India / Burma (Myanmar) / Sri Lanka** as a category 1 hurricane. On 2 May it had become a category **2 / 4 / 5** hurricane and made landfall on the coastline of Burma (Myanmar). It travelled across the country in a **north-easterly / south-westerly** direction and eventually ended on 4 May.

4 Cyclone Nargis was very destructive. The table below describes some of its features and some of its effects.

a) Colour the features of the storm in green.

b) Colour the effects of the storm in red.

Cyclone Nargis was formed over water with a temperature of at least 26°C.	An estimated 300,000 people were killed.	The wind speed reached 215 km/hr.	Three-quarters of health centres in the region affected by the cyclone were damaged.
The low air pressure caused the ocean to bulge upwards in a storm surge.	The storm surge flooded the coastal areas destroying housing and rice crops.	The strong winds created very large waves which were 7.6 m high on top of the storm surge.	About 800,000 homes were damaged.
Many people had to live with family members because they had been displaced.	There were food shortages because crops had been destroyed by the flooding.	The hurricane brought very heavy rainfall to Burma (Myanmar).	People got diarrhoea from drinking water which had been contaminated with sewage.

Review what you have learned

I can:

- identify features on a weather map ☐
- describe three facts about the track and strength of Cyclone Nargis ☐
- describe three effects of Cyclone Nargis. ☐

Case study: Drought in Barcelona

In these activities you will:

- describe the weather features of a high pressure system;
- develop a case study of drought in Barcelona.

See Student's
Book pages
90–95

1 High pressure (an anticyclone) creates different features in the weather during the summer and the winter. Read page 90 and study Figure 29 on page 93. Match up the features with the correct statements to describe anticyclones by drawing a line between them.

In an anticyclone, air pressure is …	… calm and moves at low speeds.
In an anticyclone, the air is …	… cold and dry with clear skies and frost at night.
In an anticyclone, the wind is …	… high, usually above 1020 mb (millibars).
In an anticyclone, wind moves in …	… a clockwise direction.
In a winter anticyclone, the weather is …	… sinking and becoming warmer.
In a summer anticyclone, the weather is …	… warm and dry. Heat waves are common.

2 Study Figure 32 on page 95. Complete the sentences below using words from the box to describe the location of Barcelona.

Tarragona	**Marseille**	**Rhone**	**France**	**Spain**	**Zaragoza**
Mediterranean	**Llobregat**	**Segre**	**Catalonia**	**Aragon**	**Ebro**

Barcelona is a city in the north-east of the country of .... in the

region of .... It is located on the mouth of the River

.... It is located on the coastline of the Mediterranean Sea and is

north-east of the city of ....

3 In 2007–2008 Barcelona suffered from a severe water shortage following a period of high pressure weather. Read page 94 and complete the table below.

	Evidence / example
Water use was restricted in public places.	
People who broke drought order rules were fined.	
The city was desperate and had to bring water from outside the area into the city's port.	

4 Study Figure 33 on page 95. It examines the different viewpoints surrounding the water shortage situation in Barcelona. Use this information to help you complete the following sentences.

The swimming pool manufacturer is unhappy with ....

because ....

....

The householder thinks that one reason for the water shortage is ....

because ....

....

The climate expert is against the idea of ....

because ....

....

The protestor in France is against the idea of ....

because ....

....

5 What do you think the authorities in Barcelona should do to reduce the risk of a severe water shortage in the future? Explain your ideas giving three clear points based on information on pages 94–95.

Review what you have learned

I can:

- describe three weather features of a high pressure system ☐

- describe the location of my case study (Barcelona) using a compass and scale line ☐

- describe three ways that people in Barcelona were affected by drought. ☐

Arctic ecosystems

In these activities you will:

- show you know how living and non-living things are linked in the Arctic ecosystem;

- explain the reasons for slow plant growth in the Arctic.

See Student's Book pages 98–101

1 Study Figure A and the labels below. It shows the ways that living and non-living things are linked together in an Arctic ecosystem. Write the number of each label into the correct box in Figure A.

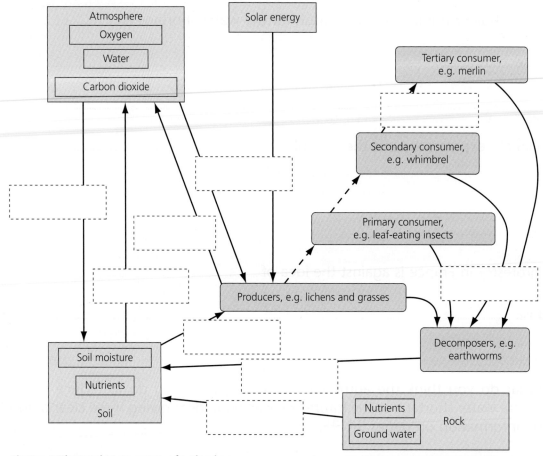

Figure A The tundra ecosystem of Iceland

1 Precipitation	2 Evaporation
3 Weathering of rocks releases nutrients into the soil	4 Plant roots take up water and nutrients from the soil
5 Decomposition breaks down dead matter and the nutrients are released into the soil	6 The loss of water from pores in the leaves of plants (known as transpiration)
7 Dead plant and animal matter	8 Carbon dioxide is taken into leaves and converted to starch by photosynthesis
9 Flow of energy through the food chain	

Labels for Figure A

2 Plants in Arctic ecosystems grow very slowly. Complete the following sentences to explain why they are so slow growing. Use words from the box below and the glossary to help.

nutrients	leaching	transpiration	decomposition
photosynthesise	leaf litter	slowly	quickly

Winter days are short and dark so plants are unable to .... In many

months, water is frozen in the soil so plants have small leaves to reduce water lost

through .... Bacteria in the soil reproduce very slowly in the cold

weather so .... of dead plant matter is very slow. So nutrients are

transferred from .... into the soil very .... The

chemical reactions that release .... from rocks into the soil are slow

because of the cold temperatures.

3 Study Figure B. It shows a food web in the Arctic ecosystem of northern Norway.

a) Add arrows to the diagram to show that:

i) reindeer eat lichen and moss

ii) Arctic fox eat lemming and young reindeer.

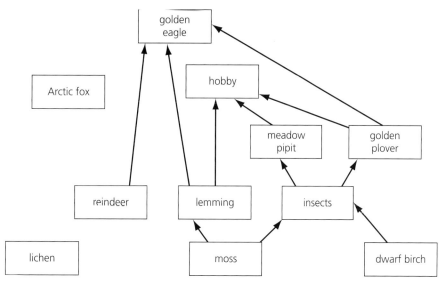

Figure B Food web in Arctic Norway

✎ **b)** Lemmings have a lot of young and breed quickly. Suggest what will happen to other living things in the food web if:

i) the population of lemmings gets very large

ii) the lemming population grows so large that it runs out of moss (which grows very slowly).

Review what you have learned

I can:

- identify three living and three non-living parts of an Arctic ecosystem and describe how they are linked ☐

- give three reasons for the slow growth of plants in the Arctic ☐

- describe an Arctic food web. ☐

Tropical ecosystems

In these activities you will:

- show you understand how water is recycled in the rainforest
- explain the reasons for rapid plant growth in the rainforest.

See Student's Book pages 102–105

1 Study Figure 17 on page 105 and Figure A below. These diagrams show how water is recycled through the tropical rainforest.

a) Match the labels to the diagram by writing the correct number in each box.

b) Colour the water stores in blue. Colour the water flows (the processes that move water from one store to another) in red.

c) Make a key for your diagram.

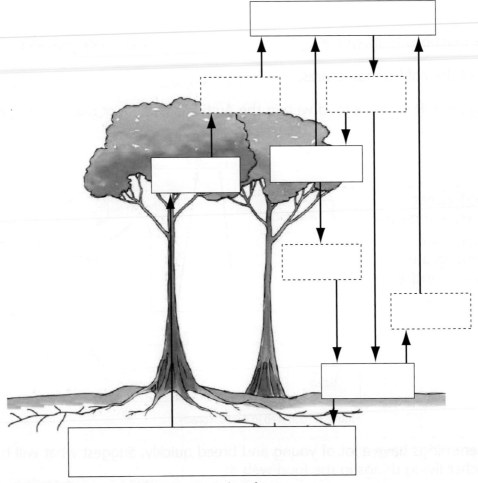

Figure A Water stores and flows in a tropical rainforest ecosystem

1 Evaporation	2 Evapotranspiration	3 Moisture in atmosphere
4 Water in the leaves and trunk of the tree	5 Moisture in the soil	6 Raindrops intercepted by the canopy
7 Stem flow and drip flow	8 Precipitation	9 Water in puddles and rivers (surface stores)

Labels for Figure A

2 Plants in the tropical rainforest grow very quickly. Complete the following sentences to explain why they grow so quickly. Use words from the box below and Figure 14 on page 103 to help you.

nutrients	leaching	transpiration	decomposition	rapid	slow
weathering	photosynthesise	soil	rocks	slowly	quickly

The winter months are warm and sunny so plants are able to ....

all through the year.

Bacteria in the soil reproduce very .... in the hot weather so

.... of dead plant matter is very rapid. So ....

are transferred from leaf litter into the .... very quickly.

The chemical reactions that release nutrients from .... into

the soil are .... because of the heat. This process is known as

.... If trees are cut down, heavy rainfall can wash nutrients out of

the soil. This process is known as ....

3 a) In each row, circle the odd one out.

					Common theme
1.	Mangrove forest	Cloud forest	Tropical rainforest	Boreal forest	
2.	Lion	Orangutan	Howler monkey	Boa constrictor	
3.	Canopy	Nutrient	Buttress root	Drip tip	
4.	Tobago	Brazil	Ghana	Iceland	
5.	Evaporation	Interception	Photosynthesis	Stem flow	

b) For each row, state what the three remaining words have in common. Write your answer in the final column of the table.

Review what you have learned

I can:

- identify three stores and three flows of rain water through the tropical rainforest ☐
- give three reasons for the rapid growth of plants in the tropics. ☐

Effects of rainforest deforestation

In these activities you will:

- consider the effects of cutting down or burning large areas of forest.

See Student's Book pages 104–107

1 Study Figure 19 on page 106. Complete the following sentence. Use words from the box in your answer.

canopy	interception	raindrops	slope

If the forest is clear felled all the trees are cut or burned. The soil is at risk of erosion

because ....

....

2 Study Figure 22 on page 107 and Figure A below. It shows how rivers can be damaged by logging.

Figure A Logging next to a river in Borneo

  a) Complete each of the labels below. The first one has been done for you.

  b) Then match the labels to locations A, B, C and D on Figure A.

Letter	Label
	Large machinery may leak oil / diesel into the river so … *the drinking water of people living downstream is polluted.*
	The remaining trees are an ecological island so…
	Soil has been washed into the river so …
	Trees next to the river have been felled and the canopy has gone so …

3 If very large areas of rainforest are cleared, this can affect the water cycle and even begin to affect the local climate patterns. Choose statements from the box below and add them to Figure B.

Less rainfall   Eroded soil may wash into rivers   Less water vapour in the air
Rain hits ground with more force   Less cloud formation

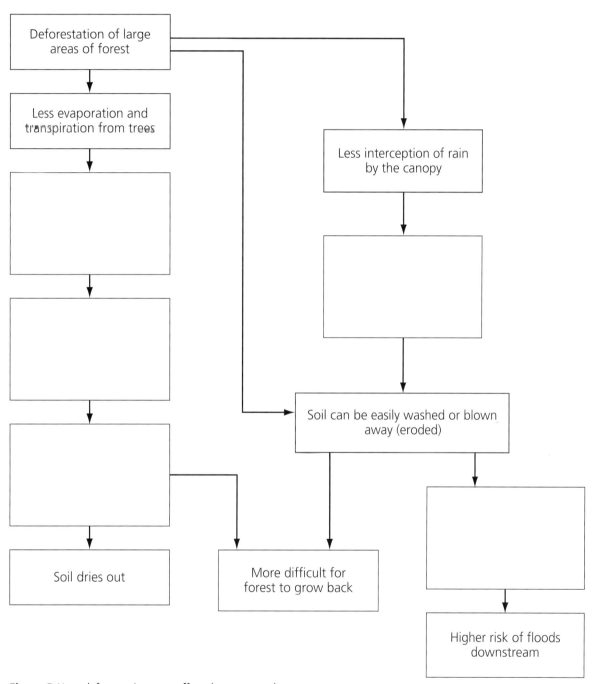

Figure B How deforestation may affect the water cycle

Review what you have learned

I can:

- explain why deforestation leads to soil erosion ☐
- describe how deforestation can affect local climate. ☐

What processes are involved in desertification?

In these activities you will:

■ show you understand the causes of desertification.

See Student's Book pages 120–125 and 128

1 Match the following key words to their definitions in the table below.

a) Desertification   **b)** Infiltration   **c)** Splash erosion   **d)** Gulley erosion

Key word	Definition
	A process by which dry environments become more like a desert
	A process by which rainwater cuts deep channels in the soil
	When heavy rainfall causes soil particles to be washed away
	Rainwater trickling into the soil and replacing soil moisture

2 In some parts of the world, where rainfall is already low, the soil is becoming worn out. When it does rain, the rain washes the soil away. Where is this happening? Study Figure 1 on page 120. Complete the following sentences.

The largest area of existing desert is .... in Africa. To the south of

this is a region at risk of desertification known as ....

Apart from in Africa, the largest regions at risk of desertification are:

■ North of the Tropic of Cancer in ....

■ either side of the Tropic of .... in Australasia.

3 Is desertification caused by people or by physical processes? Discuss each of the seven statements below. Put the numbers 1 to 7 in the correct places on the Venn diagram in Figure A below.

1. Farmers allow their goats to overgraze shrubs and vegetation is killed.	5. The rain in the wet season is unpredictable and can be very heavy causing soil erosion.
2. Annual rainfall totals are gradually falling.	6. Commercial farms use the land so intensively that the soil is quickly worn out.
3. Trees and shrubs are burned to clear land for farming or urbanisation.	7. Less vegetation means less water is returned to the atmosphere by evapotranspiration.
4. Trees are cut down for firewood for cooking.	

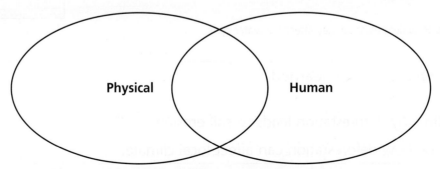

Figure A Physical and human factors that may cause desertification

4 Study Figure 8 on page 125. It shows a deep gulley that has been eroded in the soil. Complete the description of the gulley by using words from the box below.

transportation	erosion	deposition	attrition	abrasion	downwards
diagonally	sideways	speed up	slow down		

The gulley has been formed by .... The water has cut

.... into the soil. One way it has done this is by using small rocks

to cut into the soil, a process known as .... The farmer is placing

stones across the gulley to .... the flow of water during the next

rain storm which should encourage the .... of soil in the gulley.

5 Study Figure 14 on page 128. It describes some of the causes of desertification in northern Ghana. Use information from this diagram to complete the table below. You will need to:

a) underline increases or decreases in the middle column;

b) finish the sentences in the final column to complete each explanation.

Causes of desertification ———→	So ... ———————→	Which means that ...
Arable farmers and agri-businesses use the land more intensively now ...	The length of the fallow period ... **increases / decreases**	The soil dries out and ...
The urban population is growing and few families have electricity ...	The amount of firewood needed for cooking ... **increases / decreases**	Trees ...
Cattle farmers are more settled than they used to be ...	The same areas of land are grazed and the amount of grass and shrubs ... **increases / decreases**	There are fewer plants so ...
There are fewer shrubs and trees ...	The amount of moisture given off by evapotranspiration **increases / decreases**	The amount of moisture entering the atmosphere ...

Review what you have learned

I can:

■ describe three main regions of the world that are at risk of desertification ☐

■ explain three causes of desertification. ☐

Case study: Desertification in northern Ghana

See Student's
Book pages
126–131

In these activities you will:

■ develop case study notes;

■ consider the views of stakeholders;

■ weigh up the usefulness of one solution to the problem of desertification.

1 Northern Ghana can be used as a case study of a region that is suffering from desertification. You need some facts for your case study.

a) Read pages 126–129.

b) Complete the following statements about the problem of desertification in Ghana.

The largest city in northern Ghana is …	The average income in northern Ghana is less than US$ …
The natural vegetation in northern Ghana is …	Trees have been cut down in northern Ghana to …
The risk of soil erosion in the Northern and Upper West regions is …	The northern regions of Ghana face severe social problems such as …
Most people cook using …	Farmers remove natural vegetation using a technique known as …
A large amount of crop land is now used to grow biofuel crops. One such crop is …	The estimated amount of cropland used to grow biofuels in Ghana is …

2 Different people (stakeholders) have different views about growing biofuel crops.

a) Underline the correct answers in the following sentences:

Biofuel crops are processed to produce **food / vegetables / oils**. This is then used

to replace **cooking fat / heating oil / diesel**. The European Union has set a target to

get **10 / 20 / 30** per cent of transport fuels from renewable sources by 2020.

b) Read Figure 16 on page 129. Which stakeholder:

i) feels pushed off her land? ....

ii) is concerned that the fallow period is too short? ....

iii) thinks that biofuels need too much water and pesticides? ....

3 One way to help solve the problem of desertification could be to cook on more fuel efficient stoves. Read page 131 and complete the following sentences:

Traditional cooking stoves burn **coal / wood / gas**. They use **a little / a lot of** fuel

for the amount of heat energy they give off. The Upesi stove uses **more / the same**

amount / less wood to make the same amount of heat. It can be made **abroad / by**

machines / by local women using **imported / local** materials.

4 Discuss the nine benefits of the Upesi stove shown in Figure A below.

a) Decide whether each benefit is a social, economic or environmental benefit. Colour each box and complete the key.

b) Place each of the benefits into the diamond nine diagram (Figure B). Put the benefits you think are most important at the top of the diamond.

1. Women spend less time collecting firewood.	6. Using less firewood means trees have longer to recover.
2. Women have fewer injuries to their back and neck.	7. The women who make the stoves learn new skills and earn respect.
3. Women and children have a reduced health risk.	8. Women earn an income from making and selling the stoves.
4. Cooking is faster and cleaner, producing less harmful smoke.	9. The stoves have lower CO_2 emissions than a traditional stove.
5. The clay used to make the stoves is collected locally.	

Figure A The benefits of the Upesi stove

Key

☐ Social benefits
☐ Economic benefits
☐ Environmental benefits

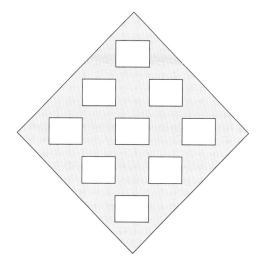

Figure B Diamond nine diagram

5 Explain why you think the Upesi stove might help. Focus on social, economic and environmental benefits.

Review what you have learned

I can:

■ give five facts about northern Ghana ☐

■ give three benefits of the Upesi stove. ☐

River processes

In these activities you will:

- show you know how rivers can shape the land
- practise the technique of labelling and annotating a photograph.

See Student's Book pages 136–143

1 Rivers shape the landscape. They erode soil and rocks from one place. Rivers then transport this sediment along their course before depositing it to make a new landform.

a) Study Figure 2 on page 136.

b) Identify the main features of the river at labels A and C and complete the third column in Figure A below.

c) Suggest how much energy the river has at B and C (on a scale of very high to very low) and complete the fourth column in Figure A.

d) Work in pairs to suggest what processes may be happening at A, B and C (there may be more than one process at each location). Choose from processes in the box:

| deposition   saltation   hydraulic action   suspension   abrasion   attrition   slumping |

	Part of the river channel	River features	Energy levels	Possible processes
A	Outer bend		Very high	
B	Middle	Riffle		
C	Inner bend			

Figure A Features and processes in the river shown in Figure 2 on page 136

e) Use what you have learned to complete this conclusion:

At A the energy level of the river is .... The river is able to

use this energy to erode the river cliff using the processes of ....

At C the energy level of the river is .... This means that

the main processes here are ....

2 Figure 5 on page 137 shows a river that has split into several channels just as it flows into a lake. This feature is known as a **delta**. A labelled delta is shown in Figure 17 on page 142.

a) Add labels to boxes A and B on Figure B that describe the features.

b) Add annotations to boxes C and D to describe the process occurring in this delta.

B

D

A

C

Figure B The processes at work in a delta

3 Study Figures 18, 19 and 20 on page 143.

   a) Match the labels A to I on these photos to the labels and annotations below.

   b) Colour the labels in yellow and the annotations in blue.

   c) Suggest how the river feature at G may have been formed.

Letter	Label or annotation
	Water tumbles into this plunge pool with a lot of force. Sediment carried by the river scours the bottom of the plunge pool in a process called abrasion.
	River cliff
	The river here is grey providing evidence that a lot of sediment is being transported in suspension. This sediment proves that there is a lot of erosion further upstream.
	Evidence that the flow of the river in this part of the channel is very slow because a bar of sand and gravel is being deposited here.
	Steep-sided walls of a gorge. Gorges like this are often formed below a large waterfall. The gorge gets longer as the waterfall retreats further upstream.
	V-shaped valley with interlocking spurs
	Rock pinnacle or stack
	An ox-bow lake has been formed because erosion of the outside bend of the river channel has cut off the old meander. The water is now flowing swiftly through the cut-off channel and the old meander loop has been abandoned.
	Small waterfall

Review what you have learned

I can:

■ label and annotate a photograph of a river landform. ☐

How are waterfalls formed?

In these activities you will:

- practise using key words that describe river processes and river landforms;
- show you know how waterfalls are formed and how they change over time.

See Student's Book pages 136–141

1 Study the words in the box below. Some are river features; others are terms that describe the process of erosion or the transport of sediment in a river. Sort the words into the three categories. One of each has been done for you.

| abrasion   saltation   river cliff   traction   delta   suspension   plunge pool   attrition |
| solution   hydraulic action   slip-off slope   ox-bow lake   corrosion   meander |

River features	Processes of erosion	Transportation
delta	corrosion	saltation

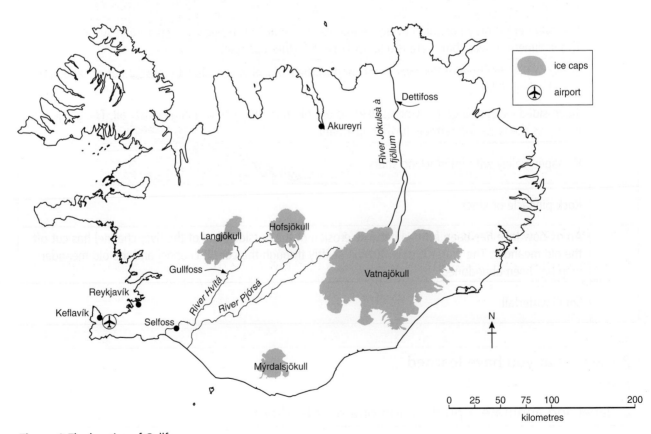

Figure A The location of Gullfoss

3 Study Figure A. Describe the location of Gullfoss: underline the correct words or complete the gaps in the passage below.

Gullfoss is a waterfall on the River **Hvítá** / **Pjórsá**. The source of this river is the ice cap

known as **Myrdalsjökull** / **Hofsjökull** / **Vatnajökull**. The river's mouth is on the **east** /

north / **south** coast. Gullfoss is .... km from Keflavik and .... km from Selfoss.

4 Figure B shows another large waterfall and gorge in Iceland close to Dettifoss.
   a) Add the labels, below, to suitable places on Figure B.

1 A layer of harder rock that is difficult to erode	**2** Plunge pool where hydraulic action and abrasion are eroding the bed of the river
3 Overhang that could collapse in the future	**4** Steep sides of the gorge formed as the waterfall retreats

Figure B Waterfall at Dettifoss

b) Describe the location of Dettifoss.

5 Now draw your own series of diagrams to show how this waterfall will change over time. Add labels that explain what is happening. Use your own words as well as those from the box below.

erosion	collapse	plunge pool	retreat	hydraulic action	gorge

Review what you have learned

I can:

- use six words to do with river processes with confidence ☐

- describe the location of a place on a map using a scale line and compass ☐

- describe how river processes can change one landform over time. ☐

Flow of water through the drainage basin

In these activities you will:

- improve your knowledge of key words to do with drainage basins
- show that you know how water flows through different drainage basins.

See Student's Book pages 146–149

1 Match the following key words to their definitions in the table below.

a) Precipitation   e) Infiltration   i) Groundwater flow

b) Transpiration   f) Percolation   j) Interception

c) Evaporation   g) Overland flow

d) Condensation   h) Throughflow

Key word	Definition
	Water moving through the ground below the water table
	When leaves prevent water from falling directly to the ground
	The movement of water from the ground surface into the soil
	The process where water changes state from gas to liquid
	The movement of water from the atmosphere to the ground
	The downhill flow of water through soil
	Water loss from plants through pores in the leaves
	The flow of water across the ground surface
	Where water changes state from liquid into vapour
	Movement of water out of the soil and into the rocks below

2 a) Add the key words a)–j) from activity 1 above to Figure A on page 51 to show the stores and flows in a natural drainage basin.

b) Draw arrows between the key terms to show how the water moves around the drainage basin.

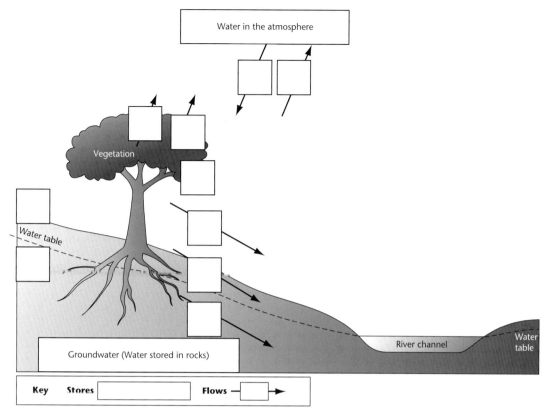

Figure A Movement of water through the drainage basin

3 Work in pairs for this activity. Study Figure 27 on page 148 and the two diagrams in Figure B. Predict which hydrograph each catchment area would produce by writing A or B in the box next to each statement.

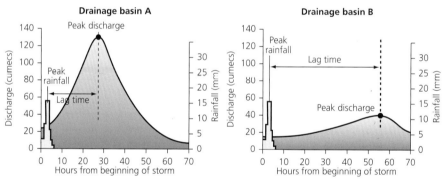

Figure B Hydrographs for two different catchment areas

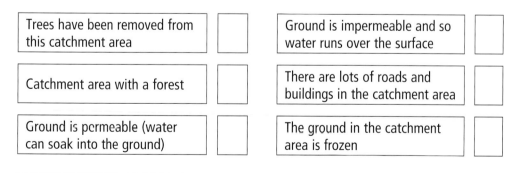

Trees have been removed from this catchment area	Ground is impermeable and so water runs over the surface
Catchment area with a forest	There are lots of roads and buildings in the catchment area
Ground is permeable (water can soak into the ground)	The ground in the catchment area is frozen

Review what you have learned

I can:

■ describe how water moves through the drainage basin.

Causes of floods

In these activities you will:

- investigate why rivers flood;
- analyse and compare two hydrographs.

See Student's Book pages 150–153

1 Match the following key terms to features on the map in Figure A. Write the correct letter next to the feature.

   1. Catchment area = ...
   2. Confluence = ...
   3. Source = ...
   4. Tributary = ...
   5. Watershed = ...
   6. Mouth = ...

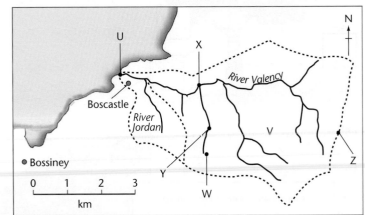

Figure A The drainage basin of the River Valency

2 The water level in the River Valency rose very quickly during the flood of 2004.

   a) Study Figure 30 and Figure 31 on page 150.

   b) Use the information in the orange boxes in Figure 31 to complete the middle column in Figure B below.

Reasons for the sudden rise in water level of the River Valency	Effect on the flow of water in the area (choose from the orange boxes in Figure 31)	Map evidence (use information from the box below to help)
Narrow valleys		
Small areas of woodland		
Steep slopes		
Impermeable underlying rock		
Upland areas are very close to Boscastle		

Figure B Features of the drainage basin of the River Valency

   c) Study Figure 30 on page 150 and the statements in the box below. Match each of these statements to the correct box in the final column of Figure B.

> **Map evidence to help suggest why the River Valency flooded in 2004**
>
> **A** = Land in square 0989 is 240m above sea level and is only 1km from Boscastle.
> **B** = Deciduous trees found in 1091.
> **C** = In square 1191, the contour lines are very close together.
> **D** = Narrow valleys funnel water, for example in grid square 1290.
> **E** = There are lots of streams in the area, for example the River Valency has six tributaries.

3 Read the information on page 152 and underline the correct answers in the sentences below.

Hydrographs record the **evaporation / infiltration / discharge** of a river. They may be used to help organisations like the Environment Agency to predict flooding.

The geology of the River Dyfi is 100 per cent impermeable rocks which means water **does / does not** soak into the ground easily. In contrast, the geology of the River Itchen is 90 per cent chalk which allows water to soak into the ground so the Itchen is **less / more** likely to flood than the Dyfi. The land around the River Dyfi has steep slopes so it is **more / less** likely to flood because there will be a **rapid / slow** rate of overland flow. Water is taken out of the **River Dyfi / River Itchen** for water supply which reduces the discharge.

4 a) Study the hydrograph on page 153. Complete the sentences below using words from the box.

anticyclones	40	depressions	snow	400	high	6th
low	rising	sinking	rain	120	180	165
				3rd		

From 7 to 13 January there was a series of .... over Wales and the Midlands which led to wet weather. This type of weather event happens when the air has .... pressure and is .... and cooling which leads to clouds and rain. On 15 January, the rainfall was .... mm and the discharge of the River Severn was .... cumecs. By 17 January the discharge had increased to .... cumecs. One reason for the delay between the highest rainfall and the highest discharge is that the precipitation fell as .... and so took a few days to melt and flow to the river. The highest rainfall in this period happened on .... February at .... mm. The highest discharge of the River Severn in February was on .... February at .... cumecs.

Review what you have learned

I can:

- find evidence on an Ordnance Survey map that helps to explain flooding ☐
- read rainfall and discharge values from a hydrograph. ☐

Effects of floods

In these activities you will:

- consider how flooding can have devastating effects on people and the environment.

See Student's Book pages 154–155

1 How do floods affect people and the environment? Identify the different effects of the floods in 2007 and 2012 by placing a tick (✓) in one or more columns.

		The effects of the flood were …		
		social	economic	environmental
1.	People were left without tap water after a water treatment plant flooded.			
2.	Homes were flooded and people had to move out. Some people had to live in temporary accommodation for months.			
3.	Thousands of motorists were stranded as roads became impassable and motorways closed.			
4.	Sewage pipes overflowed.			
5.	Schools were closed. Many children had their work destroyed by the floods.			
6.	Catfish (which are large predators) escaped from lakes and got into the River Severn.			
7.	Caravan sites were flooded and the caravans were damaged.			
8.	A music festival was cancelled in Coventry.			
9.	The Yorkshire Agricultural Show was cancelled.			
10.	Train services were suspended between Glasgow, Edinburgh and Carlisle due to landslips and flooding on the railway line.			
11.	An electricity substation was closed causing 40,000 people to lose electricity.			
12.	Many shops had to close down for weeks after the floods.			

2 How were different groups of people affected by the flooding? Look at the answers below which are very simple explanations. Try to improve the answers by adding more detail and explanation in the final column. Try to use the words 'so' and 'because' in your answers. One has been done for you.

Groups of people	Simple answer	Developed answer
Elderly people who live alone and rely on regular visits from friends	felt isolated.	Regular visitors, like meals-on-wheels, could not visit, so no one could check that elderly people were OK.
Emergency services like fire-fighters	were under pressure.	
Supermarkets and shops	struggled because they needed regular deliveries.	
Homeowners whose houses were damaged by the floodwater	had to live in temporary housing.	
Organisers of events like the music festival in Coventry and the Yorkshire show in Harrogate	lost money.	
Commuters	struggled to get to work by road or train.	

Review what you have learned

I can:

- describe five effects of river floods ☐
- identify three groups of people who are affected by flooding in different ways. ☐

Management of floods

See Student's Book pages 156–162

In these activities you will:

■ show you know how rivers can be managed to reduce flooding;

■ comment on the advantages and disadvantages of each management strategy.

1 The River Valency has been managed to reduce the risk of future floods. Study the features shown in Figure 43 on pages 156–157.

a) Explain how each of the features may reduce the risk of future floods. Complete the second column of the table below.

b) Label the hard engineering strategies in the table with H, and the soft engineering strategies with S. One has been done for you.

Management strategy	How it will reduce the risk of future floods	H or S?
Catchment management upstream, e.g. trimming back and removing trees from water's edge		S
Make the river channel wider and shallower just before the river enters the village		
Introduce a 'trash screen' which will stop debris like boulders, stones, trees and branches being washed into the culvert drain and blocking it		
New flood defence wall		
Widen river channel		
Lower (dig out the) river bed		
Remove lower bridge		

2 Flood management strategies have advantages and disadvantages.

   a) Use the information on pages 156–159 to complete the table below to show the advantages and disadvantages of flood management strategies.

Flood management strategy	Advantages	Disadvantages
Creating natural sections of river that will encourage deposition upstream of towns that are at risk of flooding, e.g. River Valency, Boscastle, page 156		
Straightening river channel, e.g. River Valency, Boscastle, page 156		
Having a flood plan for residents, page 158		
Building earth embankments alongside river channels, e.g. River Severn, Shrewsbury, page 159		
Having demountable flood barriers, e.g. River Severn, Shrewsbury, page 159		
Not allowing building of more homes on the flood plain, page 161		
Blocking field drains and planting trees in the upland part of the drainage basin, e.g. River Severn, page 162		

Review what you have learned

I can:

- give three facts about management of the River Valency at Boscastle ☐

- describe four different ways that rivers can be managed to reduce flooding ☐

- give one advantage and one disadvantage of one of these management strategies. ☐

Erosion at the coast

In these activities you will:
- show you know how cliffs are eroded.

See Student's Book pages 164–167

1 Study Figure 3 on page 165.

  a) Add key terms to the table below to show the different processes of coastal erosion.

  b) Draw simple diagrams in the third column to show each process in action.

Key term	Definition	Diagram
	Waves crash against the cliff, compressing the water and air into cracks and forcing rocks apart	
	Waves pick up rocks and smash them against the cliffs	
	Minerals are slowly dissolved in sea water	
	Sand and pebbles are picked up by the waves and smash against one another, breaking into smaller pieces	

2 a) Study Figure 4 on page 165. It shows how cliffs made of resistant (hard) rocks retreat when they are eroded.

  b) Match the labels for Figure A to the correct point in the diagram by adding arrows.

  c) Add a number to each label to suggest the best sequence in which to read them.

The cliff retreats leaving a wave cut platform behind.

The cliff forms an overhang over the eroded notch.

Waves use pebbles from the beach to erode a notch at the foot of the cliff.

Figure A Cliff retreat

3 a) Read the information on page 166 which describes how cliffs made of softer rocks are eroded.

b) Match the letters from Figure 5, page 166 to the correct labels in the table below.

Letter	Label
	Waves have eroded the base of the cliff
	The vegetation on this slope proves that it has not slumped for several months
	Concrete blocks on the beach may protect the cliff from wave erosion
	Evidence of gulley erosion by rain water is visible on these slopes

4 Study Figure 7 on page 167. Use words from the box below to help you write labels in the boxes around Figure B to describe what is happening in the landscape.

arch	hard rock	softer rock	resistant rock	easily eroded
eroded slowly	vertical cliff	sloping cliff	semi-circular bay	
biological weathering	slumping	limestone	clay	chalk

Figure B The erosion of Durdle Door (which is made of harder rocks)

Review what you have learned

I can:
- use, with confidence, four key words that describe the processes of coastal erosion ☐

Beach and sand processes

In these activities you will:

■ show you know how the process of longshore drift works.

See Student's
Book pages
168–169

1 Study Figures 9, 10 and 11 on pages 168–169. Use words from the box below to describe what processes may be happening at each label, A, B and C.

Beach	**sand dunes**	**wave-cut platform**	**spit**	**hydraulic action**	**abrasion**
swash	**backwash**	**attrition**	**transportation**	**deposition**	

A is a ....

It has been formed by ....

....

At B there is a long ....

It has been formed by ....

....

Over a long period of time this feature will change by ....

....

At C there are ....

These features are formed when sediment is swept up the beach and ....

....

2 Study Figure 8 on page 168 and underline the correct answers in the passage below.

The movement of sand along a beach is a process called **erosion / longshore drift / deposition**. The waves are pushed up the beach at an angle by the **backwash / wind / tide**. This is called the swash and it deposits beach material like pebbles and sand on the beach.

Some of the beach material is picked up by the waves and carried back off the beach by gravity. This is called **backwash / deposition / swash**. The swash and backwash move sediment along the beach in a zig-zag pattern.

3 The process of longshore drift has created a depositional landform known as a spit at Borth. Study Figure 11 on page 169. Use information from this diagram to complete the labels in Figure A.

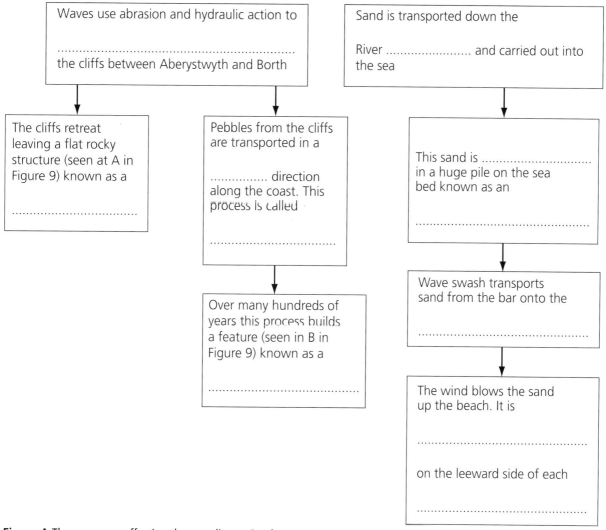

Waves use abrasion and hydraulic action to

....

the cliffs between Aberystwyth and Borth

Sand is transported down the

River .... and carried out into the sea

The cliffs retreat leaving a flat rocky structure (seen at A in Figure 9) known as a

....

Pebbles from the cliffs are transported in a

.... direction along the coast. This process is called

....

This sand is ....
in a huge pile on the sea bed known as an

....

Over many hundreds of years this process builds a feature (seen in B in Figure 9) known as a

....

Wave swash transports sand from the bar onto the

....

The wind blows the sand up the beach. It is

....

on the leeward side of each

....

Figure A The processes affecting the coastline at Borth

4 Show you understand coastal landforms and processes.

a) In each list, circle the odd one out.

					Common theme
1.	Swash	Backwash	Longshore drift	Spit	
2.	Arch	Spit	Stack	Cave	
3.	Abrasion	Deposition	Hydraulic action	Corrosion	

b) For each list, state what the three remaining words have in common. Write your answer in the final column of the table.

Review what you have learned

I can:

- describe how sediment is moved along the coast by longshore drift. ☐

Coastal management

In these activities you will:

■ describe different ways that coastlines may be managed

■ consider the advantages and disadvantages of one coastal management strategy.

See Student's Book pages 173–174, 179–185

1 a) Study each of the **six** management strategies listed in the table below by reading the page numbers (given in the first column of the table).

b) Describe how the strategy works and give a located example to complete the table (one has been done for you).

✎ **c)** Choose **one** of these strategies and describe its advantages and disadvantages.

Coastal management strategy	How it works	Location
Sea wall Figure 18, page 173 Figure 37, page 182	A large curved wall of concrete is built along the top of the beach. It reflects the energy of the waves and prevents the waves from eroding rocks by hydraulic action or abrasion.	Sea Palling, Norfolk
Wooden groynes Figure 21, page 174		
Artificial rock reef Figure 19, page 173 Figure 32, page 179		
'Sandtainer' reefs Figure 38, page 182		
Beach replenishment Page 183		
Managed realignment Figure 44, page 185		

2 a) Study the information on pages 180–181 which shows how Australia is being affected by coastal erosion and how planners are trying to manage the impacts.

b) Use the information to complete the table below.

Coastal change threatens Australia's coastal lifestyle, warns report
Thousands of miles of Australian coastline are under threat from rising sea levels.

Coastal erosion has social impacts People are worried because:	**Three** important facts:
	▪ .... ▪ .... ▪ ....
Examples of **three** places that are being affected: ▪ .... ▪ .... ▪	**Coastal erosion has economic impacts** The damage to the coastline will cause economic problems such as: ....

Different stakeholders have different views
Some groups of people are in favour of building more sea defences because:

....

....

....

Other groups of people are against building more sea defences because:

....

....

....

Review what you have learned
I can:

▪ describe three different ways to manage the coast ☐

▪ identify the advantages and disadvantages of one coastal management strategy ☐

▪ describe the views of two different stakeholder groups. ☐

Uneven Developments and Sustainable Environments

What do we mean by employment structure?

See Student's Book pages 188–193

In these activities you will:

■ show you know the difference between primary, secondary and tertiary sectors;

■ practise the technique of drawing a pie chart.

Geographers sort the jobs that people do into categories. One way is to sort them into primary, secondary and tertiary jobs. Each of these is known as a sector of the workforce.

1 Study Figure 1 on page 188. Use words from the box to complete the description below.

make things	give a service	grow food

In primary jobs, people get raw materials or .... An example is a farmer.

In secondary jobs, people .... An example is a worker in a car factory.

In tertiary jobs, people .... An example is a nurse or shop assistant.

How are employment structures changing?

The sectors of the workforce are often shown as percentages. So, the employment structure for a country can be shown as a pie chart, like Figure 2 on page 189. Figure A shows you how to draw a pie chart.

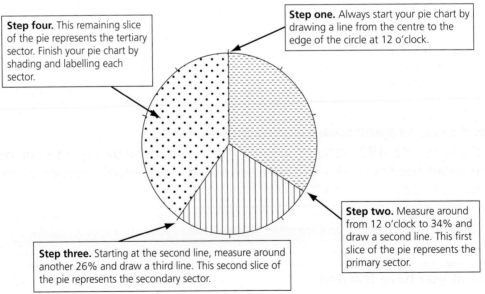

Step four. This remaining slice of the pie represents the tertiary sector. Finish your pie chart by shading and labelling each sector.

Step one. Always start your pie chart by drawing a line from the centre to the edge of the circle at 12 o'clock.

Step two. Measure around from 12 o'clock to 34% and draw a second line. This first slice of the pie represents the primary sector.

Step three. Starting at the second line, measure around another 26% and draw a third line. This second slice of the pie represents the secondary sector.

Figure A The male employment structure of Malaysia (1980)

2 Use the data in Figure 3 on page 189 to complete the two pie charts below.

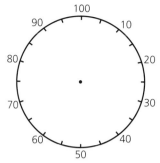

Figure B The male employment structure of Malaysia (2010)

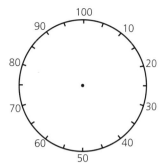

Figure C The female employment structure of Malaysia (2010)

3 Study the three pie charts on this page. Choose the best words from the box below to complete the sentences in parts a) and b).

a lot / a little   **twice as many / half**
risen / fallen / stayed the same   **fewer / greater**

a) Comparing the male employment structure of Malaysia in 1980 to 2010:

The percentage of males employed in the primary sector has decreased by ....

The percentage employed in the secondary sector has increased by ....

The percentage employed in the tertiary sector has also ....

b) Comparing the male employment structure of Malaysia in 2010 to the female employment structure In 2010:

Almost .... males as females work in the primary sector.

.... women work in the secondary sector than men. However, the

percentage of women working in the tertiary sector is .... than men.

✎ **6** Read pages 192–193 about changing jobs in manufacturing. In your own words, write about the changes in manufacturing jobs. You should include as many of the following words as you can:

Mechanisation   de-industrialisation   high-tech industries   skills   training

Also include at least two facts, two dates and two place names in your description.

Review what you have learned
I can:
■ draw a pie chart ☐
■ describe two ways that employment structures are changing. ☐

What are the differences between formal and informal work?

See Student's Book pages 194–197

In these activities you will:

- show you know the difference between formal and informal work;
- identify advantages and disadvantages of formal and informal work.

1 Study Figure 18 on page 194. Use it, and examples from the boxes below, to complete the table about jobs in Mali.

child care	selling street food
teaching	collecting water
work in a bank	collecting firewood
collecting scrap materials	

| Little protects you from injury at work |
| You earn no money and have no savings |
| You have to pay tax |

	Examples of this job	Disadvantage of this job
Informal work that is unpaid		
Informal work that is paid		
Formal work		

2 Complete the following table to show the main differences between the features of formal and informal work. Some have been done for you.

	Formal	Informal
Pay		Low and irregular
Tax		
Holidays		No paid holidays
Sick pay		
Training		No formal training. You learn on the job
Opportunities for a career		
Safety at work		

Advantages and disadvantages of formal and informal work

Having a formal job has advantages. Some advantages are for the worker, like regular pay. The country also benefits from having formal jobs. For example, people pay tax so the government gets money. They can spend this on health care or schools.

3 a) Work in pairs. Discuss the information on pages 196–197.

b) Use your ideas to complete the heads and tails exercise below. One job has been done for you.

1. I am a welder. My employer has given me a six month contract so …	… my family worry about me when I'm at work.
2. I sell food on the street. I don't have a permit for a market stall so …	… I can progress in my career.
3. I work with waste chemicals. I don't have any safety equipment so …	… I know I will be able to pay my rent and pay my children's school fees.
4. I work for a bank and I get regular training so …	… I don't have much time to rest and I am always tired.
5. I am a young mother. I spend a lot of time each day collecting water and fire wood so …	… sometimes I am hassled by the police and get moved on.

c) Now decide whether each statement describes an advantage or disadvantage of formal or informal work. Complete the table below.

Statement	Advantage / Disadvantage	Formal / Informal work
1	advantage	
2		
3		informal
4		
5		

d) Ask your partner to check your work.

4 Study Figure 23 on page 197. Use this flow chart to complete the sentences below.

a) Wages in informal jobs are very low so families …

b) Informal workers do not pay tax so the government …

c) Children stay at home to help their families so they …

5 In rural areas of Mali, women spend eight hours a day working on the farm and eight hours doing informal work. Suggest ways their lives would be improved if they had:

a) a clean water supply in the home   **c)** a health centre in the village.

b) electricity in the home

Review what you have learned

I can:

- give three features of informal work ☐

- give two advantages and three disadvantages of informal work. ☐

Location factors

In these activities you will:

- consider the location factors that attract high-tech industries;
- practise the technique of drawing and labelling a sketch map.

See Student's Book pages 198–199

1 Consider the three statements in the table below. They all describe the location factors that make **one** city on Figure 1 on page 198 attractive to high-tech industries.

a) Which city best fits all three of these statements? Circle one of the following:

    Cardiff   **Reading**   **Bristol**   **Cambridge**

b) Now add to each of the statements to explain why the location is an advantage. One has been done for you.

Location factor	Which means that ...
Heathrow airport is close by	... company directors can fly in to meetings.
2.2 million people live within easy commuting distance	
This city has a first rate university	

2 Now consider three more statements below. They all describe the location factors that make **one other** city in Figure 1 on page 198 attractive to high-tech industries.

a) Which city best fits all three of these statements? Circle one of the following:

    Cardiff   **Reading**   **Bristol**   **Cambridge**

b) Now add to each of the statements to explain why the location is an advantage.

Location factor	Which means that ...
The government encouraged foreign TNCs to invest	
The M4 motorway is very close	
There is a large container port only 50km away	

3 Use Figure 1 on page 198 to complete the following sentences. Fill in the gaps and underline the correct answers.

Cambridge is located at the end of the M ..... motorway. It is about .... km

south / west / north of London. Cambridge has a number of **high / medium / low-**

tech firms. The people who work in these firms are **high / medium / low** skilled. Their

workers are often recruited from the local ....

4 Study the OS map, Figure 3 on page 199.

   a) Complete the right half of Figure B shown below. Include the features that you think are the most important for industries in this area.

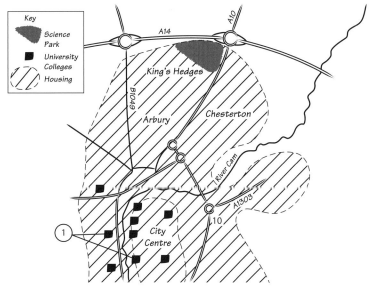

Figure B Sketch map showing the location of Cambridge's Science Park

   b) Complete each of the labels to explain why industries might want to locate here. One has been done for you.

1. Companies on the Science Park *can employ graduates from the University*.

2. The airport is useful because ....

3. There is housing nearby so ....

4. There is a junction on the A14 so ....

   c) Match each of your labels to a place on the sketch map. One has been done for you.

5 Research the location factors that influence the location of an industry. Choose one of the following industries:

   Aluminium smelting   Steel works   Motor car manufacturing

Using the writing framework below, explain why the location was chosen for the industry.

- Describe briefly the industry and location (include place names and facts).
- Explain why the location was chosen (include specific information, for example roads, rail, flat land, workers nearby, access … and more).
- Write a final summary to highlight two main reasons for the choice of location.

Review what you have learned

I can:

- describe three location factors for high-tech industries ☐
- draw a sketch map and label important features on it. ☐

Location of a tourist resort

See Student's Book pages 204–205

In these activities you will:

- use compass points and a scale line to describe a location;
- consider why Cancun is a good location for a large tourist resort;
- practise the technique of drawing a climate graph.

In the 1970s, Cancun in Mexico was a tiny fishing village. Planners decided it was the perfect location for a large tourist resort. Why?

1 Use Figure 12 on page 204 to complete the following sentences.

Cancun is in the state of **Quintana Roo / Yucatan / Belize**. It is on the coastline of

the .... Sea. It is .... km north-east of the resort of Playa del

Carmen. Chichen Itza is 220 km to the **north-west / north-east / west-south-west**.

✎ **2** Describe the location of Tulum. Use your answer to activity 1 to help structure your answer.

3 What makes Cancun a good location for a large holiday resort? Match the following statements to the factors shown on the spider diagram below. Some statements can be used twice. Two have been done for you.

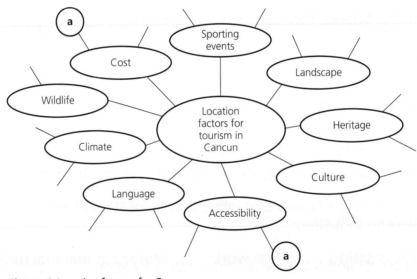

Figure A Location factors for Cancun

a It is easy to get there cheaply by air from the USA.	**f** There are plenty of places to dive on the reef.
b People can surf and water ski.	**g** Guides can take visitors turtle watching.
c It is warm and sunny for most of the year.	**h** There are miles of sandy beaches.
d People can go bird watching in the rainforest.	**i** The resort has an airport nearby.
e People can visit Mayan ruins (like Figure 13) and museums.	**j** The sea is warm which encourages water sports.

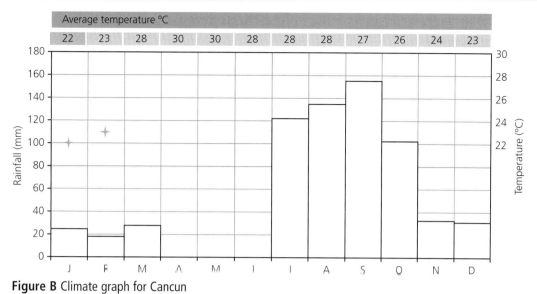

Figure B Climate graph for Cancun

4 Complete the climate graph for Cancun, shown in Figure B.

a) Add three bars for the rainfall in April, May and June, based on the table below.

	Apr	May	Jun
Rainfall (mm)	30	80	170

b) Plot points, in the middle of each month, for the temperature. The first two have been done for you.

c) Join the temperature plots with a red line.

5 Use Figures A and B and Figure 12 on page 204 to write an article on Cancun for a holiday brochure. Make sure you mention:

- climate
- beach
- water sports.
- location
- warm water

Review what you have learned

I can:

- use compass points and a scale line to describe a location ☐

- explain why the tourist resort was developed at Cancun giving three location factors ☐

- draw a climate graph with confidence. ☐

What are the advantages and disadvantages of mass tourism?

See Student's Book pages 206–208

In these activities you will:

■ show you understand key geographical terms to do with tourism;

■ describe the advantages and disadvantages of mass tourism;

■ consider whether mass tourism in Cancun is sustainable.

1 Match the following key words to their definitions in the table below.

   a) Direct jobs created by tourism

   b) Indirect jobs created by tourism

   c) Positive multipliers

   d) Enclave tourism

   e) Mass tourism

Key word	Definition
	Where the benefits of a new industry spread through the local economy
	Jobs that already exist but which benefit from tourism such as taxi drivers
	Where large numbers of tourists visit the same resort
	Where tourists are encouraged to stay in the hotel/resort
	Jobs in tourism industries such as hotel workers

 2 Read the comments made on pages 206–207. Describe the effects of each on local people or local businesses. One has been done for you.

   a) There are a lot of jobs in hotels and bars so … *a lot of people have moved to Cancun to find work.*

   b) Most jobs are unskilled and badly paid so …

   c) Tourists stay in their hotels and rarely visit local bars and shops so …

   d) Most airlines that bring tourists to Cancun are owned by American or European companies so …

Is mass tourism sustainable in Cancun?

Many people think that mass tourism in Cancun has been unsustainable. Read the list of statements below. They are based on pages 207–208.

1. Wages in bars and hotels are low.	9. Informal 'shacks' are small and overcrowded.
2. Informal workers are hassled by police.	10. Hotels use a lot of fresh water.
3. Drug and alcohol misuse are becoming a problem.	11. Informal 'shacks' are badly built.
4. The reef is damaged by boats and divers.	12. People in shanty towns have to share toilets.
5. Working hours are long.	13. Local people are not allowed on the beach.
6. The coral reef has been damaged by sewage.	14. The lagoon is polluted by oil from boats.
7. Working conditions are stressful.	15. Hotels import expensive food.
8. Rents for formal housing are very high.	16. Air conditioning in hotels uses a lot of energy.

3 Study Figure 21 on page 207 and the list on page 72. Choose at least eight statements from the list and add them to the copy of Figure 21 below to show why tourism may be **unsustainable** in Cancun. One has been done for you.

Local people need to benefit. 13	The environment should not be damaged so much it cannot recover.
The growth of tourism should not create problems for future generations of people.	The growth of tourism should not create so many problems that people stop coming.

✎ **4** Choose one statement from each box above. Write at least three suggestions about what needs to be done in Cancun to make tourism **more sustainable**.

5 Tourism in Cancun has damaged the coral reef. What do you think should be done to reduce this damage?

a) Read the nine possible solutions below and add them to the diamond shape. Put the numbers of the solutions that you think would work best at the top.

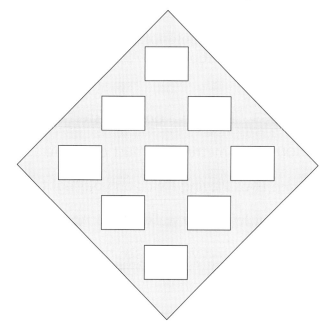

1. Allow divers to use only one section of reef.

2. Spread divers over a much wider section of reef.

3. Ban all divers from the reef for five years.

4. Educate divers about the reef system.

5. Improve sewage treatment in Cancun.

6. Make rainforest tours cheaper.

7. Make diving much more expensive.

8. Spend money on scientific research on the reef.

9. Create a new dive site by sinking an old ship.

✎ **b)** Explain why you think your chosen solutions are best.

Review what you have learned

I can:

- use key terms with confidence ☐

- describe one advantage and two disadvantages of mass tourism ☐

- give three reasons why mass tourism may not be sustainable for Cancun. ☐

Case study: Creating new habitats from a damaged environment in London

See Student's Book pages 218–219

In these activities you will:

■ practise the technique of drawing a sketch of a landscape;

■ show you know how environments can be repaired and restored.

1 Read the text on pages 218–219 and refer to the glossary on pages 274–280 to help you match the following key words to their definitions in the table below.

a) Brownfield site   **c)** Greenfield site   **e)** Leisure activity

b) Economic activity   **d)** Habitat   **f)** Reservoir

Key word	Definition
	A plot of land that has not been built on before
	A plot of land that has already been built on or used
	An artificial lake where water is stored for human use
	Actions that create wealth such as farming, manufacturing or retailing
	Sports and recreational activities carried out in people's free time
	The plants and landscape that make a home for wildlife

2 Look at Figure 15 on page 218. Complete the following sentences to describe how a visitor would get to the Wetlands Centre from Barnes Station (223756) by underlining the correct answers.

Leave the station and walk along the **A306 / A3003 / B306** in a **north-easterly / south-westerly** direction. After about **100 / 500 / 900** metres you must cross the B439. After another 200 metres you will see Barn Elms Playing Fields on your right and you will see **the river / housing / a school** on your left. Keep walking in a **northerly / southerly / westerly** direction for another 300 metres and you will see the entrance to the Wetlands Centre on your **left / right**.

3 Creating the Wetland Centre at Barn Elms turned a brownfield site into a more natural environment. Sort the statements and copy them into the correct column of the table.

a) All water at the same depth   **d)** A wide variety of habitats

b) Water at different depths   **e)** Lots of ducks

c) Only one kind of habitat   **f)** More types of insects, fish and other birds

Before the restoration	After the restoration

Deeper water with submerged vegetation provides …	The lake edge provides …

An island provides …	Shallow water with emergent vegetation provides …

Figure A Sketch of the London Wetlands Centre

4 a) Use Figure 16 on page 219 to complete the drawing of the wetland centre by adding some details to the right of the sketch.

b) Complete each of the four labels using the statements in the box below. Your finished labels will explain why this is a good habitat for wildlife.

> 1. a safe place for birds to nest away from predators like foxes
> 2. sites for dragonflies to lay their eggs
> 3. a good place for moisture loving plants like rushes
> 4. food for diving ducks and a safe place for dragonfly larvae

c) Draw arrows connecting the labels to the correct places on your finished diagram.

d) Add a caption to your drawing that gives one way that people benefit from these new habitats.

5 Research a brownfield site near to your school. Suggest how it could be restored to benefit wildlife **and** people.

Review what you have learned

I can:

- draw and label a sketch of a landscape ☐
- describe three ways that Barn Elms, a derelict landscape, has been improved. ☐

What is the greenhouse effect?

In these activities you will:

- describe the stores and flows of the carbon cycle;
- show you know the difference between causes and effects of climate change.

See Student's Book pages 220–221

1 Carbon dioxide is a greenhouse gas. In order to understand the greenhouse effect we need to understand the carbon cycle. Study Figure A and the labels below the diagram.

a) Sort the labels into two types:

- carbon stores
- flows between stores

Colour the stores and flows labels using two contrasting colours and complete the key.

b) Add the number of each label to the correct place on Figure A.

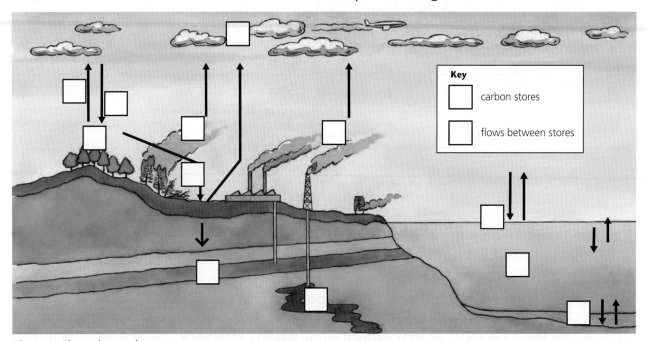

Figure A The carbon cycle

1. Fossil fuels, such as coal, gas and oil, store carbon for very long periods of time	**2.** Burning fossil fuels releases CO_2
3. Plants take in CO_2 during photosynthesis	**4.** Trees store carbon for hundreds of years
5. Decomposition of leaves / branches returns carbon to the soil	**6.** Living things breathe out CO_2 (respiration)
7. Burning trees releases CO_2	**8.** CO_2 dissolved in the ocean
9. CO_2 in the atmosphere	**10.** CO_2 moves between the ocean and atmosphere
11. Dead plant matter is compressed and turns to rock (lithification)	**12.** Dead algae and seashells contain carbon

2 Show you understand the carbon cycle.

   a) Study each of the following lists of words. In each list, circle the odd one out.

					Common theme
1.	Fossil fuels	Forests	Atmosphere	Respiration	
2.	Cars	Airplanes	Wind turbines	Coal-fired power station	
3.	Photosynthesis	Respiration	Coal	Decomposition	
4.	Wind energy	Coal	Oil	Gas	
5.	Oxygen	Carbon dioxide	Methane	Water vapour	

   b) For each list, state what the three remaining words have in common. Write your answer in the final column of the table.

3 Increasing the amount of carbon dioxide in the atmosphere seems to make the greenhouse effect stronger. This may be one explanation for recent climate change.

   Cause or effect? Read each statement in the table below. Decide whether it is a potential cause or effect of climate change. One has been done for you.

	Cause (C) or Effect (E)
Heating our homes by burning gas or coal	C
Burning coal in a power station	
Unusual weather	
Chopping down large areas of tropical rainforest	
More floods of coastlines	
Generating electricity by burning fossil fuels such as gas	

	Cause (C) or Effect (E)
Increasing numbers of flights	
Sea levels rising	
Ice melting in Greenland	
Burning coal in a factory to make steel	
More hurricanes and storms	
Increasing numbers of cars on the roads	

✎ **4** Study Figures 20 and 21 on page 221. Describe two ways that cutting down or burning large areas of tropical rainforest will affect the carbon cycle.

Review what you have learned

I can:

■ describe flows and stores in the carbon cycle   ☐

■ give two causes and three effects of climate change.   ☐

How could climate change affect people in the future?

See Student's Book pages 224–225

In these activities you will:

- study two cities that are at risk of sea level rise and flooding
- practise the geographical technique of drawing and analysing a bar graph.

✎ 1 Explain why New Orleans is at risk of future flooding. Arrange the following phrases into a sequence to help you. Choose some connectives from the box below to join your phrases together.

so	therefore	which means that	however	because

- large parts of New Orleans are below sea level
- New Orleans is at high risk of flooding in the future
- the soft sands are drying out
- the city is built on a delta deposited by the River Mississippi

- land in the delta is sinking
- sea levels have been rising by about 2 mm every year
- sea levels may rise by 4 mm a year in the future.

2 Scientists believe that climate change will lead to stormier weather.

a) Use information in Figure 26 on page 225 to complete the empty boxes in the table below.

← Stronger hurricanes

	Category 5	Category 4	Category 3
Air pressure (mbs)		920–945	
Wind speeds (km/hr)		211–250	
Risk of coastal flooding			Low risk
Damage from wind	Roofs of large industrial buildings blown off		

b) Underline the correct answers in the paragraph below.

Category 5 hurricanes are the **weakest / strongest** type of storm. With today's level of CO_2 category 5 hurricanes are rather rare. For example, when the air pressure is 900 mbs there are about **5 / 20 / 30** occurrences each year.

With extra CO_2 in the atmosphere, category 5 hurricanes will become **more / less** common.

When air pressure is 900 mbs there may be about **5 / 20 / 30** occurrences each year.

The rising threat of flooding in the Thames estuary

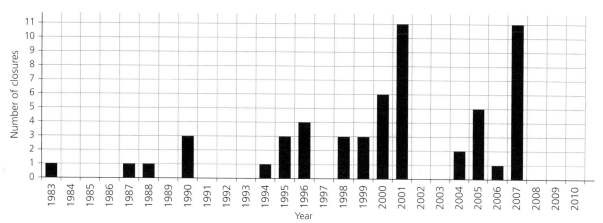

Figure A Number of closures of the Thames Flood barrier

3 Complete the graph of closures of the Thames flood barrier using the data below.

Year	1992	1993	2002	2003	2008	2009	2010
Number of closures	1	5	2	8	3	5	5

4 Complete the sentences below. Fill in the gaps and underline the correct answers.

The Thames barrier was closed .... times in the first ten years (1983–1992). It was

then closed **35 / 38 / 41** times in the next ten years (1993–2002). The largest number

of closures in any one year was in .... and ....

The number of closures each year has been **going up and down / steadily**

decreasing / staying the same, and there were significantly **more / fewer** closures in

the 2000s than in the 1980s.

5 Do some research into one of the following cities. Explain why your chosen city is at
risk from climate change.

    a) Mumbai (Bombay), India   **c)** London, UK

    b) Dhaka, Bangladesh

Review what you have learned

I can:

- draw and analyse patterns from a graph ☐

- name two places in the world that are at risk of tropical
  storms and floods ☐

- explain the connection between greenhouse gas emissions,
  global warming and increased risk from weather hazards. ☐

Why is it important for girls to complete their education?

See Student's Book pages 236–237

In these activities you will:

- show you know why it is beneficial for girls to complete their education;
- practise the geographical technique of drawing a shaded (choropleth) map.

In some parts of South Asia, girls miss a lot of school. This means a lot of young women cannot read and write properly. This causes serious problems. For example, the child of an uneducated mother is twice as likely to die before the age of one as a child whose mother has a full education.

1 Study Figure 10 on page 236 carefully. It shows the advantages that an educated mother has compared to a mother who was not able to finish school.

   a) Close the textbook! Now complete Figure A below by adding words from the box in each blank space. You may use words more than once.

| better | lower | earlier | higher | fewer | later | sooner | less | worse |

   b) When you have finished, check your answer by looking at Figure 10 on page 236 again.

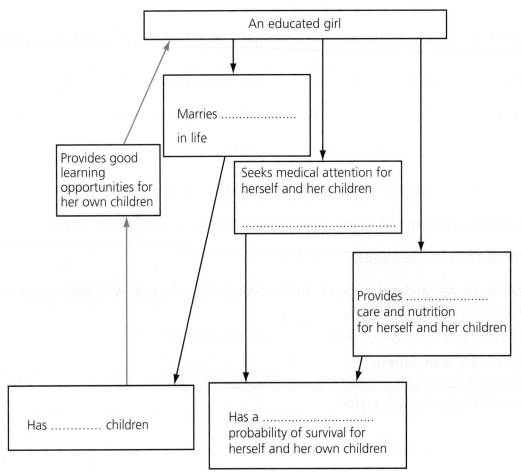

Figure A The future advantages of educating girls

✎ **2** Use Figure A to complete each of the following statements.

▪ An educated mother spots the early signs of ill health in her child so …

▪ An educated mother understands the importance of a balanced diet so …

▪ An educated mother recognises the importance of a full education for her daughter so …

3 Use the data in Figure 12 on page 237 and Figure B below to make a map showing female literacy in India.

   a) Choose four colours for the key. Use the lightest colour for the smallest numbers.

   b) Colour each state on Figure B using your key. For example, Andhra Pradesh has female literacy of 50.4% so it fits into the range 45%–59.9%.

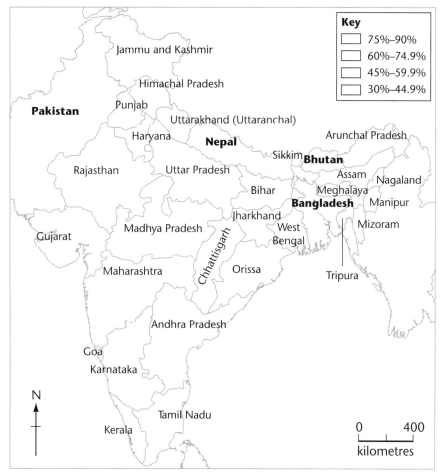

Figure B Outline map of the states of India

✎ **4** Compare your finished map to Figure 11 on page 237.

   a) What are the similarities between the two maps?

   b) What does this tell you about the importance of education for girls?

Review what you have learned

I can:

▪ give three reasons why girls should complete their education ☐

▪ draw a shaded (choropleth) map and analyse the pattern that it shows. ☐

Investigating development data

In these activities you will:

See Student's Book pages 236–237

- practise the geographical technique of drawing a scattergraph
- make predictions and investigate relationships.

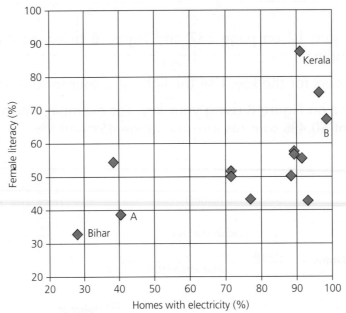

Figure A Investigating the relationship between homes with electricity and female literacy in Indian states

Figure A is a scattergraph. A clear pattern on a scattergraph may indicate that two sets of data are linked in some way.

1 Figure A has been drawn using data from Figure 12 on page 237. The graph plots data for the first fourteen states in the table from Andhra Pradesh down to Madhya Pradesh.

a) Use information in the table to identify the states A and B.

State A is ....

State B is ....

b) Complete the following sentences about Figure A.

States which have few homes with electricity have **low / medium / high** female

literacy. An example is .... States which have many homes with electricity

have **low / medium / high** female literacy. An example is ....

c) Suggest a reason for the pattern shown in Figure A. Tick (✓) one of the following answers to show the most likely reason:

☐ Homes with electricity have better lighting so children can do their homework.

☐ The poorest homes have no electricity. Families in these homes are so poor they cannot afford to send their daughters to school.

☐ Some Indian states do not have enough money for either schools or electricity connections.

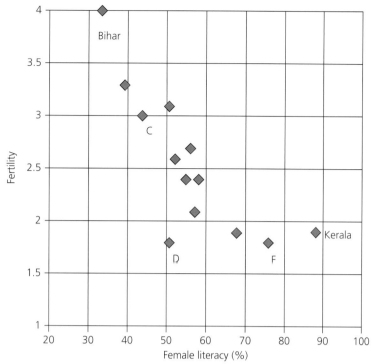

Figure B Investigating the relationship between female literacy and fertility

2 Figure B has been drawn using data from Figure 12 on page 237. The graph plots data for the first fourteen states in the table from Andhra Pradesh down to Madhya Pradesh.

a) Use the table to identify the states C, D and E.

State C is ....

State D is ....

State E is ....

b) Complete the graph by adding ten more states from Figure 12 on page 237.

c) Complete the following sentences about Figure B.

States which have low female literacy have **low / medium / high** fertility. An example

is ....

States which have high female literacy have **low / medium / high** fertility. An example

is ....

Review what you have learned

I can:

■ draw a scattergraph ☐

■ make predictions and use a scattergraph to investigate relationships. ☐

Water and health

In these activities you will:

- practise the geographical technique of drawing divided bars;
- describe how water supply can affect health and quality of life.

See Student's Book pages 242–245

1 Water is needed for a healthy life. But many families in the world's poorest countries do not have enough clean water. Read pages 242–243 . Match the following key words to their definitions.

a) recharge **b)** aquifer **c)** abstraction **d)** over-abstraction

Key word	Definition
	Porous rocks under the ground that contain water
	When people remove water from the ground, a reservoir or a river
	When rainwater replaces water that has been taken out of an aquifer
	When too much water is taken from the ground and the aquifer dries out

2 Use the data in Figure 5 on page 244 to complete two divided bar charts in Figure A for:

a) the savanna regions of Northern Ghana **b)** all of Ghana.

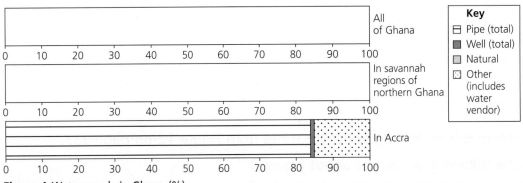

Figure A Water supply in Ghana (%)

3 Complete the following description of the graphs by underlining the correct answer and filling in the gaps using words from the box below:

wells	natural sources	pipes

In Accra most people get their water from .... whereas in the savanna

regions most people get their water from .... In all Ghana about

16 per cent get their water from .... whereas in the savanna regions this

percentage is **half / twice / three times the amount.**

✎ **4** A poor water supply can affect quality of life. Use the words and phrases in the box below to help complete each sentence to suggest how a poor water supply might affect a family.

| expense | neck or back pain | wasted time | lack of privacy | sickness |

a) Many women and children carry water long distances to their homes so ... and ...

b) People in shanty towns may have to buy water from a private seller in the street so ...

c) People use streams for washing and collecting water so ...

d) Some wells are unprotected from animal waste so ...

e) Families who have no water supply have very small amounts of water for washing so ...

✎ **5** How could the water supply be improved in:

a) Accra   b) the savannah regions of northern Ghana?

6 Study Figure 6 on page 245 which shows a graph.

a) Complete the following description of the graph by underlining the correct answers.

In 1990 the percentage of the population of the Arab states with access to safe water was **80 / 83 / 85** per cent. Over the next twelve years this had risen to **84 / 86 / 88** per cent. It seems **likely / unlikely** that this region will reach its target of **88 / 90 / 92** per cent with access to safe water by 2015.

b) Compare the progress made in each region between 1990 and 2002 with the progress needed between 2002 and 2015 to decide whether each region is likely to reach its target. Put a tick (✓) in the column that you predict.

Region	Likely to reach target	Unlikely to reach target
World average		
Arab states		
Latin America and Caribbean		
East Asia and the Pacific		
South Asia		
Sub-Saharan Africa		

Review what you have learned

I can:

■ draw a divided bar graph ☐

■ describe two ways that water supply can affect health and quality of life. ☐

Case study: Water supply in South Africa

In these activities you will:

- show you know why it rains in Lesotho more than in South Africa;
- describe advantages and disadvantages of the LHWP.

See Student's Book pages 246–253

The pattern of rainfall in South Africa is very uneven. Most rain falls in the mountains in the east. This region includes Lesotho, a small country that is entirely surrounded by the much larger South Africa.

1 a) Study Figure A below.

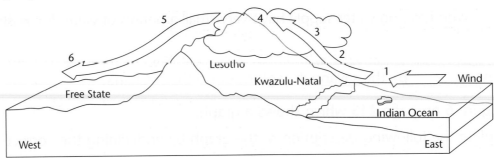

Figure A Diagram of rainfall patterns

b) Use words from the box to complete each label (1–6) for the diagram.

Evaporates / condenses prevailing / shadow	leeward / windward leeward/windward	descends / ascends

1. Water vapour .... from the warm Indian Ocean. This moisture is picked up by the prevailing wind.

2. Air rises up the .... slope of the mountains in KwaZulu-Natal.

3. As the air .... it cools. The water vapour .... into small water droplets.

4. Water droplets bump into one another. Clouds form and it rains in Lesotho.

5. The air crosses the mountains. The temperature rises as the air ....

6. The air on the .... side of the mountains is now warm and dry. This is called the rain ....

The Lesotho Highlands Water Project (LHWP)

The government of Lesotho agreed to sell some of its water to South Africa. Dams have been built to collect the water. Tunnels take the water through the mountains into South Africa. It then flows down rivers towards Johannesburg where it is used.

2 What are the advantages and disadvantages of the LHWP? Read the statements opposite (based on evidence on pages 248–249).

a) Sort the statements by colouring advantages in green and disadvantages in red.

b) Decide whether each statement describes an advantage/disadvantage for Lesotho or South Africa. Add L (Lesotho) or SA (South Africa) to the final column.

Advantages (green) and disadvantages (red) of the LHWP	L or SA?
Lots of construction jobs were created when the dams and tunnels were built.	
The percentage of people with a safe water supply in this country has increased.	
In the future, illness caused by drinking dirty water should be very rare.	
People in Johannesburg paid higher water bills to help pay for the LHWP.	
This country receives income from selling water to the other. The LHWP earns 75% of the country's income.	
Income from the LHWP could help this country develop its own water management schemes in the future.	
Local people have not had any of the water for their own homes.	
Farmland was flooded when the dams were built.	
Losing so much farmland may make it difficult for this country to grow enough food in the future.	
If the project is completed it will affect the quality of river water. Wildlife may be affected by lower oxygen levels and colder water temperature.	
The dams provide cheap hydro-electric power (HEP).	
The government of this country had to borrow US$8 billion to pay for the dams and tunnels. This money will take many years to repay.	
Many people lost their homes when their land was flooded by the new dams.	
Improved roads were constructed to gain access to the dam sites.	
Around 20,000 people moved into informal settlements to work on the dams. Social problems such as HIV and alcoholism became an issue.	

✎ 3 Look at your completed table above. Overall, do you think the LHWP was a good water project for **both** countries? Explain your decision.

✎ 4 The LHWP is a large-scale water management project. It was very expensive. Use pages 252–253 to investigate small-scale, cheap ways of managing water. Make a poster that describes how these projects work. Explain their advantages.

Review what you have learned

I can:

- explain why it rains in Lesotho ☐

- give one advantage and one disadvantage of the LHWP for Lesotho. ☐

Globalisation

In these activities you will:

■ consider the benefits and problems of globalisation for India;

■ compare the imports and exports of Ghana and the UK.

See Student's Book pages 258–265

We are all connected to people in other parts of the world. Ideas, money and information connect us. The process of globalisation is what makes the world more connected.

1 Cause or effect? Read each statement in the table below. Decide whether it is a potential cause (C) or effect (E) of the process of globalisation. One has been done for you.

	C/E		C/E
The invention of the internet		Faster, larger airplanes	C
We can buy tropical fruits in the UK		Satellites that improve communications	
Growing demand for expensive goods in NICs such as India and China		People watch Hollywood films in Asia	
Electronic transfer of money		People watch Bollywood films in the UK	
The growth of mobile phone systems		Companies open factories or offices in different countries	
We can buy raspberries in winter		People migrate within Europe to find work	

2 Do you think that Tata is good for India?

a) Read the statements below about their new car, the Nano. They are based on the information on page 261.

b) Decide where each statement fits best to complete the table on page 89. One has been done for you.

1. Poor families ride on scooters which can be dangerous. The Nano means that families will have a safe form of transport.

2. The Nano is cheap. It will be affordable to millions of Indian families.

3. The Nano produces very little pollution compared to other vehicles in Indian cities.

4. The Nano uses very little fuel.

5. There is too much traffic in Indian cities. Tata's new car will make traffic jams worse.

6. The Nano is clean, but there will be so many of them that air pollution will get worse.

7. People in West Bengal did not want Tata's new factory. They would have lost their land but would not have got jobs in the factory.

8. The Nano will be sold to other developing countries which will be good for India's pattern of trade.

9. As Indians get wealthier the demand for new cars will grow. So, even more jobs will be created.

	Benefits for India created by Tata's success	Problems for India created by Tata's success
Economic		
Environmental		
Social	1	

✎ **3** Use Figure 3 on page 260 to describe how workers in Europe will benefit if the Tata Nano is successful. Include facts and place names.

4 Read pages 264–265. Match the following key words to their definitions.

   a) quotas   **b)** primary commodities   **c)** social premium   **d)** import duty

Key words	Definitions
	Restrictions on the amount of particular goods that can be imported each year
	A tax placed on goods brought into a country to make them more expensive
	A small payment made by Fairtrade companies to their suppliers that is then used to fund community projects
	Raw materials which have not been processed

5 Study Figure 9 on page 264. Underline the correct answers in the sentences below.

Ghana's exports are largely agricultural products; they make up **33% / 43% / 53%**

of all exports. However, in the UK, primary commodities form a **smaller / larger /**

similar percentage of the exports. Ghana's largest import is **agricultural / mining /**

manufactured products and these make up about **55% / 65% / 75%** of all imports.

✎ **6** Use Figure 10 on page 265 to complete each of these sentences.

   a) Cheap food grown in Europe is sometimes exported to Africa so farmers in Ghana …

   b) The price of cocoa beans goes up and down so farmers in Ghana …

   c) In 2006 the EU placed a quota on the number of shoes that could be imported from Asia so workers in China and Vietnam …

Review what you have learned

I can:

- describe one benefit and one problem of globalisation for India   ☐
- describe Ghana's pattern of trade.   ☐

Ghana and the cocoa trade

See Student's Book pages 264–269

In these activities you will:

- show you know how cocoa farmers' incomes are affected by supply and demand;
- describe the benefits of Fairtrade.

Around 1.6 million people in Ghana grow cocoa. Cocoa is Ghana's second most important export after gold.

1 Complete the following flow chart using the words *decreases* or *increases*.

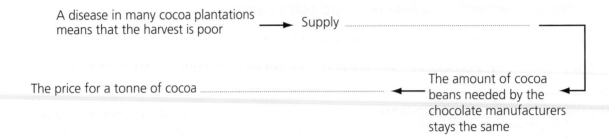

A disease in many cocoa plantations means that the harvest is poor ⟶ Supply ....

The price for a tonne of cocoa .... ⟵ The amount of cocoa beans needed by the chocolate manufacturers stays the same

2 Most cocoa is grown on very small farms. Some of the farmers have joined together to get a fair price for their cocoa. They also get money called a **social premium** that can be used to fund a community project like a new well. Cocoa is grown in the south and west of Ghana where the climate is hot and wet.

a) Use Figure 20 on page 269 and Figure B below to make a coloured map showing borehole and hand dug wells funded by the social premium.

b) Which part of Ghana has benefited most from the social premium?

....

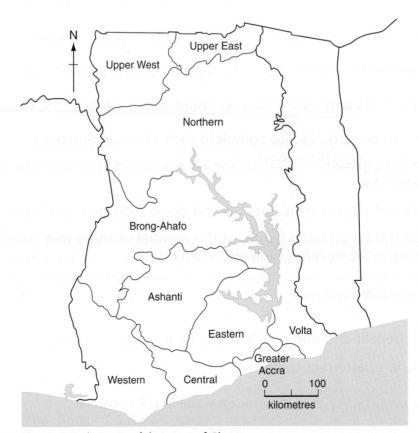

Figure B Outline map of the states of Ghana

3 Study Figure A. Complete this spider diagram by adding labels from the choices below. One future prediction has been made for you.

supply decreases	supply increases
demand decreases	demand increases
the price of Ghana's cocoa decreases	the price of Ghana's cocoa increases

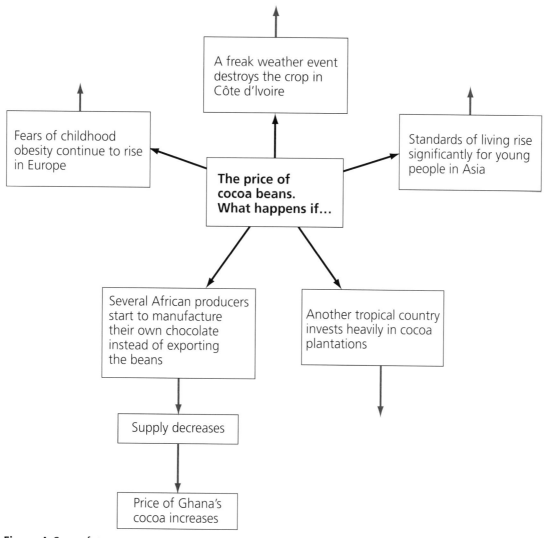

Figure A Cocoa futures

✎ **4** Design a poster for Year 7 students in your school. It should describe the benefits of Fairtrade for farmers in Ghana. Include the following: a logo, two facts, a place name, names of producers or companies involved in Fairtrade. Refer to page 268 and Figure 20 on page 269 for information.

Review what you have learned

I can:

- describe how cocoa farmers' incomes are affected by supply and demand. ☐

Notes